More Wandering Back-Roads West Virginia

with Carl E. Feather

*Volume II of the
Wandering Back-Roads West Virginia with Carl E. Feather series*

More Wandering Back-Roads West Virginia
By Carl E. Feather,
Author of *My Fathers' Land* and *Mountain People in a Flat Land*
Wandering Back-Roads West Virginia Series Volume II

Published by The Feather Cottage
6 Seaford Lane, Bruceton Mills WV 26525
thefeathercottage.com / carl@thefeathercottage.com
Copyright 2024 Carl E. Feather / Feather Cottage Media.
Registration Number TX 9-390-448.
"Wandering Back-Roads West Virginia" is copyrighted by Carl Eugene Feather.

All rights reserved. No part of this book may be reproduced in any form or by any electronic or mechanical means, including information storage and retrieval systems and audio books, without permission in writing from the publisher, except by reviewers, who may quote brief passages in a review.

ISBN: 978-1-7330460-6-0 (paperback)
Library of Congress Control Number (LCCN): 2024905043

GOLDENSEAL magazine is a publication of the West Virginia Department of Arts, Culture & History, The Cultural Center, 1900 Kanawha Blvd. E., Charleston WV 25305-0300

Printed and bound in USA
First printing, March 2024

AI was not used to produce the contents of this book.
All photos in this book, unless otherwise attributed, are by the author, Carl E. Feather, and copyrighted.
Front cover photo: From Chapter 2, Jim Davis, Cunningham Run, Harrison County, April 2007.

Other books by Carl E. Feather

Mountain People in a Flat Land:
Appalachian Migration to Northeast Ohio, 1940-1965
Ohio University Press

Covered Bridges of Ashtabula County, Ohio
Hidden History of Ashtabula County, Ohio
Arcadia

Ashtabula County: A Field Guide

Ashtabula Harbor, Ohio:
A History of the World's Greatest Iron Ore Receiving Port

Pleasure Grounds: 150 Years of Geneva-on-the-Lake,
Ohio's First Summer Resort

My Fathers' Land: Palatinate Immigration
to North-Central West Virginia

Wandering Back-Roads West Virginia (4 volumes)

Wandering Tucker County, West Virginia

Wandering Route 50, West Virginia

A Gathering of Feathers (Lenox Memorial Cemetery Feather burials)

Feather Cottage Media

Order Feather Cottage Media books online at
books.by/feather-cottage-media

Dedication

To Ruth, my wife:

Who saw something in a broken man worth redeeming,
stood by him when his world turned against him,
brought him to the mountains,
walked with him through the valley of the shadow of death,
restored him back to health,
and never once gave up on our vision for this series.

Acknowledgments

Several of the stories in this book were originally published in the pages of GOLDENSEAL magazine, West Virginia Department of Arts, Culture and History. The author is grateful for their ongoing support of my work and the publication's focus on the people and stories of traditional life in West Virginia. Over the decades, I have had the privilege of working with some of the finest people and editors in the business: Ken Sullivan, John Lilly, Stan Bumgardner, and current GOLDENSEAL editor, Laiken Blankenship.

Lemley Mullett, photographs manager at the West Virginia and Regional History Center of West Virginia University Libraries, quickly filled my requests for historical photographs used in this volume. Thank you for your professionalism and assistance, as well as maintaining an amazing resource.

A big thank you goes to my wife, Ruth, for her patience and support of all my projects and books. Each day with you is a blessing from God.

I am likewise grateful for my father, Carl J. Feather, whose support of our work makes it happen year after year.

And thank you to all the people in this book, whose stories were patiently shared and images recorded during my back-roads wanderings. Your perseverance and kindness continue to amaze me; your friendships and the experiences I had with you will be treasured as long as I have breath.

Contents

Introduction		11
1.	Hurley's Heaven	13
2.	The Iron Man	31
3.	Yokum's Vacationland	63
5.	Silas Kirk's Century	76
6.	Two Centuries	90
7.	Mail Call in Glady	95
8.	The Punch Jones Diamond	111
9.	The Wiseman of Mabie	124
10.	Railroad Cross-ing	139
11.	Wheeling's Paradox	142
12.	Mount Wood Dentist	152
Bibliography		157
Index		159
About the author		169

Introduction

This is the second book in the *Wandering Back-Roads West Virginia with Carl E. Feather* book series. As with the first book, this one relates a variety of stories discovered along the (mostly) back roads and byways of The Mountain State. Some of these stories appeared in the quarterly magazine, GOLDENSEAL, in shorter form, while others are seeing print for the first time. All of them focus on the people of West Virginia.

Whereas the first book was a rainbow of diverse characters, the stories in this book are more focused on the indefatigable spirit of the Mountaineer. I'm talking about hard times. We've all had them, or will, especially if you grew up or live in Appalachia. Mining coal, cutting timber, subsistence farming, industry—they are all hard jobs. Even more difficult is when the mines close, the last tree is harvested, the factory jobs are sent overseas, frost kills the crops, or the breadwinner suffers a heart attack.

These are things that test our mettle, that reveal our inner core. The most creative of us find ways to turn lemons into lemonade and do more than survive—we innovate and eventually prosper to face even more trials.

Mountain folks are, by necessity, resilient people. Perseverance is in their German, Scotch-Irish, and Italian genes. My father, who grew up in Preston County during the Depression, is tough as nails at 91. He still drives, takes care of more than two acres of property, and religiously feeds his wild birds, squirrels, and deer. His stamina and activity level put mine to shame. Because we know we are tough, we wear that "hillbilly" label with pride.

The folks you'll meet in this book did more than survive the storms of life. They rode them productively, making the best of what they had and leaving the rest up to the Good Lord. In the process, they gave the state some genuine, fascinating attractions and traditions: Yokum's (Seneca

Rocks) Vacationland, O'Hurley's Store, Calvin's Place, Singin in the Hills, art, Wheeling's Paradox Book Store, and large families that have carried on the heritage of perseverance.

Robert F. Kennedy, speaking on the steps of the West Virginia Capitol June 20, 1963, observed that, "The sun doesn't always shine in West Virginia but the people do." It was raining that day, as it often does in The Mountain State and life itself. That didn't keep the stouthearted people of West Virginia from celebrating the 100th anniversary of its statehood. More than sixty years later, in the 161st year of The Mountain State, it still rains in West Virginia—and its people still shine.

I pray that their light will shine through these stories as a memorial to the Mountaineer's grit, character, and heritage.

Chapter 1

Hurley's Heaven

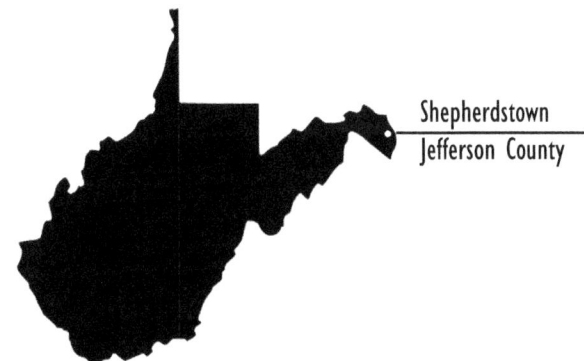

Shepherdstown
Jefferson County

During my wanderings in West Virginia, I have experienced moments so sublime that they indeed felt like "almost Heaven."

Sunrises at Dolly Sods are among those experiences. The orange orb tosses aside night's foggy blankets and frolics across the scarlet landscape of icy lace on scarlet huckleberry foliage. Those awakenings are akin to the smell of hazelnut coffee brewing and licks from the tongue of a Golden retriever puppy pouncing on flannel sheets after a night of blissful slumber. These are among the moments I would save in Jim Croce's time bottle if such a thing existed. Should heaven disappoint by being less than Dolly Sods at sunrise, I would open that bottle and experience those sunrises again. Alas, to do so would introduce the curses and mysteries of time and death into heaven, neither of which have a place in paradise, however we imagine the place.

Unfortunately, in 2023 death claimed the founder and inspiration for another of my near-heaven experiences in West Virginia: The dulcet strains of a string ensemble playing traditional tunes in The Great Hall of O'Hurley's General Store ,205 East Washington St., Shepherdstown.

O'Hurley's General Store on Washington Street in Shepherdstown has been a fixture in the town since the early 1900s. Jay Hurley carried on the tradition after his founder/father passed away.

Twice I have experienced this ethereal assembly of musicians jamming in a circle amid O'Hurley's merchandise and memorabilia, in a room designed and built by its owner, Jay Hurley. When more than a dozen musicians blended their plucked, bowed, and hammered stings into a single strain of "Shenandoah," it became a musical incense offered to the god of Appalachia. "Heaven itself must be opening a gate by which this refrain will enter," I thought. I am not ashamed to admit that tears still come to my eyes when I think of that place and the music these folks made because of Jay Hurley.

I met Jay as most folks do, by wandering into his general store during a visit to Jefferson County's Shepherdstown. I love Shepherdstown. Sited on the Potomac River, Shepherdstown is a rare holdout against corporate America's fixation with profit centers that reek of mediocrity, banality, greed, and the legalized abuse of consumers and their financial and physical well-being. That kind of riffraff is outside the town limits; within Shepherdstown proper, the community embraces an atmosphere of centuries-old architecture, history, and even retailing. O'Hurley's General Store epitomized

Jay Hurley seated at his hammered dulcimer in The Great Hall, a gathering place for the musicians who have jammed at O'Hurleys for decades. Photo from December 2014.

the latter, as it had done since "forever," when Jay Hurley's father, Milburn Glenn "M.G." Hurley, opened the business.

I returned to O'Hurley's as a writer and photographer in the spring of 2014 and spent the day and evening with Jay. As we began our interview, a Norfolk Southern freight train rumbled past the store on tracks just 50 yards away. The incursion did not faze Jay; he grew up "hearing the roar of steam locomotives on this line."

"I was born 150 feet from the tracks," Jay said, referring to his home birth April 15, 1941. This proximity provided a front seat to railroading as he watched the locomotives pass, their firemen feeding the behemoths' voracious bellies, steam and smoke bellowing from their throats. Curious about the engineering of these beasts, Jay was soon asking questions like, "Why does the smoke come from the opposite end of the engine?" and "Why does it make a 'poof, poof' sound rather than a continuous roar?"

Jay's childhood was difficult, and there was rarely money for travel beyond Shepherdstown. But he recalled a glorious boyhood moment when

Thursday evening in O'Hurley's, April 2014. Robert "Doc" Thatcher worked at the counter pricing merchandise and visiting with a local while the rest of the staff and a good many residents of Shepherdstown were in The Great Hall, jamming or listening to the music.

his mother took him and his two brothers to the railroad depot about two blocks from their home and purchased four tickets to the next stop. He recalled the thrill of crossing the Potomac River on the high-level bridge near his home and experiencing the river from an eagle's perspective.

"And then we got off the train and walked home, about four miles," he said.

Jay had no interest in taking over his father's store or staying in Shepherdstown after high school. He worked on farms around the area, then headed off to Charleston, where he earned a degree from DeVry Institute and dabbled in radio for several years. His DeVry training resulted in a job with General Electric, which assigned him to maintaining a remote radar site in the Aleutian Islands. Next came an assignment in Turkey, where he was "adopted by a Moslem" family. From there, Jay worked in the automotive industry in Michigan.

Jay Hurley had a deep respect for the history and heritage of Shepherdstown, founded as Mechlenburg. It was incorporated in 1762, and shares the honor with Romney of being the oldest incorporated towns in the state. He pauses in the town's German cemetery to read the inscriptions on the old markers.

That summary does little justice to the varied experiences, education, interests, and travels of Jay Hurley during his years of wandering the globe. Among the skills Jay acquired in these journeys was driving a team of oxen. On July 4, 1976, Jay Hurley, riding in a pilgrim's cart, drove a team along Constitution Avenue for the nation's Bicentennial Parade in Washington, D.C. That and other experiences of dabbling in his ancestors' skills, crafts, and memorabilia prepared Jay for his roles of shopkeeper, craftsman, and musician when he returned to Shepherdstown and took over O'Hurley's.

Attention to detail

In 1978, M.G. Hurley was terminally ill; Jay's brothers had no interest in continuing the store. Trading his peregrinations for a lifestyle of duty and potential mediocrity, Jay picked up the mercantile mantle of his parents and became their caretaker. He disposed of his investments in Michigan and returned to Shepherdstown with $20,000 to his name, money that he invested in revamping the store to a late-1800s ethos.

"Dad died 1 ½ months after I got here," Jay said. "I spent the first year collecting the materials I'd need to rebuild the store."

Jay spent half of his life savings on the renovation, most of which he did himself with help from college kids whom he paid $1 an hour.

"But the most difficult part was spending $10,000 on merchandise," he told me. "I'd never run a store, but I knew the kind of store that I wanted. … It was two to three years of living on cheese and crackers. Any (cash) that came in went into more merchandise."

Jay's criteria for O'Hurley's merchandise included nothing made of plastic, including the packaging. He gladly paid a premium for a similar item made of metal or wood, or one crafted by an artisan rather than a machine in China. He dealt with more than 150 craftsmen and suppliers to achieve the quality and mix of merchandise that defined O'Hurley's.

"I could see in my mind the merchandise that I wanted in my store," he told me. "It's all merchandise that you would expect to see in a general-store atmosphere. I wanted useful, functional, and non-plastic."

Jay told me that one of the nicest compliments he ever received about his store came from a woman who attended the grand re-opening.

"She stood in the middle of the doorway and said, 'Attention to detail,'" Jay recalled. "It was a well-placed compliment. I will go the extra measure to get the detail I want."

Attention to detail and authenticity also applied to the store's interior, which meant real wood fixtures and shelving. His father gave him the foundation in woodworking to make it a reality. M.G. Hurley was an accomplished carpenter and woodworker whose basement workshop was well equipped with hand and power tools despite the fact he was blind. Jay recalled a night he heard the power saw running and went downstairs to find his father operating it in total darkness.

"Dad tried to make a carpenter out of me, but he failed," Jay said, although the quality of his workmanship on the store and cabinets he built belied his modesty. Jay was more confident with metal. One aspect of his renovation work involved building a spacious metal-working shop at the rear of the store. Lathes, drills, presses, and other metalworking

Jay Hurley's attention to detail was evident in every aspect of his store, which carried good from another era, merchandised in the general-store tradition.

equipment, much of it vintage, filled the shop along with a blacksmith furnace and welding gear.

The shop was the birthplace of several projects of lasting benefit to Shepherdstown and its people. He and other volunteers restored the clock tower and weather vane of McMurran Hall. Traveling about the country

Jay Hurley in his workshop, where he fabricated the signs that welcome visitors to Shepherdstown.

and visiting small towns in search of merchandise for his store, Jay noticed that many of the communities expressed their pride with beautiful welcome signs. Jay implemented the same in Shepherdstown, and the metal signs that mark entrance to the community were birthed in Jay's fertile mind and matured by the heat of his forge and strength of his arms. The most impressive of them marks the entrance to the old industrial section and makes extensive use of iron and stone, the very building blocks of Shepherdstown.

He also spearheaded construction of a half-scale model of the steamboat that James Rumsey demonstrated on the Potomac River on December 3, 1787, 20 years before Robert Fulton's incarnation debuted (Rumsey used the less-efficient jet propulsion engine). The Rumsey half-scale model was secured in a building near the store. Jay served as a guide to store patrons who inquired about the boat, but also was known to trustingly hand over the key, provide directions, and hope for the best.

This key hung in the shadow of a bison's head with a pipe stuck in its mouth. Upon asking Jay about the beast, the raconteur launched into a long hunting story, which ended with one hunter saying to the other, "I've been hunting all my life, but that's the first time I've ever seen a buffalo smoke himself to death."

Robert "Doc" Thatcher, who worked in the store several days a week, explained that Jay's sense of humor and gift of gab resulted from laying a kiss on the Blarney Stone. The claims of Doc, in his mid-70s when I visited, required a pinch or two of salt, as well. He said he took the job because he worked 50 years in retail, and he "didn't feel like working real hard and I don't." But he loved the job, as did the store's manager, Genevieve O'Laughlin.

Doc worked meticulously, with the same attention to detail that Jay possessed. I watched him pull Christmas merchandise from a box that had recently arrived at the shop in May. He wrote the price and a brief description of each item on a tag or sticker, then attached it to the merchandise and returned it to the shipping container. Doc explained that the merchandise would not go on the shelves until after Thanksgiving. If he had his say in the matter, none of it would hit the shelves until two weeks prior to Christmas, as merchandising was done in the olden days.

"He is trying to create the feel of a late-19th/early-20th century general store," Doc said. "And I think he has done a marvelous job. Everybody calls it an antiques store. I tell them that the only antique in here is me."

Doc was tending the counter that evening, as he did most every Thursday. Jay, Genevieve, and more than a dozen local musicians and several dozen audience members, were in The Great Hall, wherein that heavenly, old-time music was performed and savored.

"(It is) about friends getting together with friends," Jay said of the sessions, which got underway 7:30 p.m. "I'd say we've missed only a couple of dates in all these years."

The sessions started as a few friends jamming behind the store counter. The first Thursday night that he issued the invitation, Jay found himself doing a solo event on his hammered dulcimer. "And it was just me for quite a while," he said.

Dave McDaniels, a guitar player, was the first to join him. Then a well-known local fiddle player, the late Walter Paton, came into the fold.

The group continued to attract musicians, some from just down the street, others from across the Potomac River or a neighboring county or

Musicians from West Virginia and Maryland crowd into The Great Hall for a jam session in April 2014.

state. As the ensemble grew, so did the audience. Soon, Jay needed a bigger space.

He built the O'Hurley's Great Hall in the 1990s to accommodate both more merchandise and jam-session players and listeners. Roger Nair, a West Virginia timber-frame expert, assisted with the design, which used queen-post, timber-frame construction. Jay turned to his stockpile of timber for the project—he'd dismantled four barns and built five, two of which he was willing to take credit for.

"I like barns, I appreciate them," he said. "When someone says to me, 'You can have this barn,' I'm going to take it. I hate to see a barn go to waste."

The same was true for bricks, fireplace lintels, siding, mobile home frames, hardware, and just about any other material that could be salvaged from a demolition. Jay felt that a divine force guided construction of The Great Hall because "when I really needed something that was important to this project, it would show up."

For example, Jay needed bricks for the massive fireplace, plus the expertise to build it. He found his material in the basement of an 1828 house

The Great Hall decked out for Christmas, December 2014. The room provided extra merchandising space for the store.

that a developer had demolished four years earlier. The salvaged, oversized bricks languished in the weather before Jay found a worthy application.

A friend assisted him with the fireplace construction; Jay traded two days of helping the friend dismantle a log house for one day of the mason's work on the fireplace. The resultant hearth required a lentil longer than the standard length. And another friend came to the rescue.

"I told him what I needed, and he said he had this lumber that had come out of a house near Harpers Ferry. He said it wasn't good enough to use on one his jobs, but too nice to throw away. He owed me a claw-foot bathtub, anyway," Jay said. To make the disintegrating wood fit for its new assignment, Jay reinforced it with 1.5 gallons of epoxy.

About the time Jay was preparing to put a floor in the hall, he heard of a massive white oak tree that had toppled onto a backyard. Jay harvested enough lumber from that tree to supply most of the hall's floorboards. He went about it the hard way, however. Jay wanted each 5/4 board the exact length of his room, 32 feet. After much searching, he found in Urbana, Virginia, a mill that could cut the log almost to his specification —only

A passionate preserver of history, Jay helped build the replica of Rumsey's steamboat that was demonstrated on the Potomac River near Shepherdstown, December 3, 1787, 20 years before Fulton demonstrated his design.

an inch or two at each board's end required hand tools to reduce the raw lumber to the desired thickness. To transport the log to the sawmill, Jay turned to his welding skills and modified a mobile home frame that a pickup could pull.

Using hand tools, Jay cut the grooves and tongues for the flooring. He built a series of sawhorses that could support the 32-foot-long pieces that the mill extracted from the log.

Why not simply piece the flooring laterally with smaller lengths, as most floors are done?

"There are a lot of things that are important to me that are not important to others," he said.

The Great Hall measures 28-by-32 feet. A huge chandelier with arms of wrought iron and a center post of solid oak, carved in the shape of an acorn, bears myriad low-wattage light bulbs that bathe the plaster-and-wood walls with luminous warmth. Smaller lamps sporting price tags provide secondary lighting. Three flags—North Ireland, South Ireland,

On Thursday evenings, Genevieve O'Laughlin traded her store management duties for a harp, which she played in the jam sessions.

and Scotland—hang from the ceiling. Queen-post trusses soar above the room and impart a sense of security, peace, timelessness, and hospitality.

Musicians sat on wood folding chairs arranged in an oval; a piano was parked against the wall opposite the fireplace, where a row of rockers provided premium seating for early birds. Three rows of gray folding chairs encircled one side of the musicians' circle; a second section of brown chairs offered additional spectator seating near the fireplace, the room's heat source in the winter.

It cost spectators and musicians nothing but their time to attend. Abiding by the rules was the only requirement. Musicians had to leave their instrument cases in the room next to The Great Hall. Only public domain songs were authorized for performance because Jay did not want to rankle ASCAP, which "would love to take us to court," Jay said.

Performers took turns selecting a song from the list of approved music that Jay compiled, although composers were permitted to perform their own works. Audience members were allowed to talk only during breaks in the music.

The Great Hall hosts some of the finest string musicians in the tristate area. Other instrumentalists joined them on occasion. It was always a sweet sound.

A hand-written sign on a small piece of cardboard was posted at The Great Hall entrance from the store: "Thou shalt not stand in doorway," with a biblical reference to Dut: 6:24. Jay said if one person stood in the doorway, a second one invariably cozied up to him and started talking. Soon, the passage was blocked.

"My overriding guideline is that if it is OK for one person to do it, it is OK for everyone to do it. And what would happen if everyone did it?" he asked.

The rules ensured that the evening flowed smoothly and safely. As host and organizer of this tradition, Jay dealt with infractions and addressed conflicts.

"I don't allow dirty blues playing and I don't allow the pendulum to swing the other way to evangelism," he said. He recalled one evening when a young man, on fire for God, attempted to turn the session into a revival meeting.

Jay Hurley and his store manager, Genevieve O'Laughlin, at their famous counter, December 2014.

"Everybody was pretty much not wanting any part of Jesus by the time it was over," Jay said.

"My biggest fear is that some hot-shot musician will dominate the session," he told me. "We had that happen in the past where a big-shot violin player started to dominate the sessions . . . I tried to have a talk with the lady, but she wasn't hearing me. Finally, she found some other place to play, and as soon as she did, things got much better here."

The group has been blessed with well-respected musicians over the years, including *GOLDENSEAL* Editor John Lilly and the late Sam Rizzetta of Inwood. Sam was a nationally recognized teacher, composer, author, innovator, and builder of hammered dulcimers.

Only acoustic instruments were accepted, with banjos, mandolins, fiddles, dulcimers, and guitars at the group's core. Genevieve played the Celtic harp, and one musician commanded so many different instruments, he hung them on a "tree" to keep them handy during the session.

Jay Hurley with his hammered dulcimer in The Great Hall, December 2014. Jay's passion for music, attention to detail, historic preservation, Shepherdstown, and learning intersected in this room.

Jay modestly said his role in the jam was "environmental control," but he was its heart and soul. Doc, tending the store while Jay immersed himself in the jam session, enjoyed the music from his perch at the sales counter.

"I love the music," he said, glancing up from his labors. And he loved the people who made O'Hurley's an Eastern Panhandle treasure.

"The people I work for are marvelous people," Doc said. "Really fine people."

On November 27, 2023, Jay Hurley died in the bedroom in which he was born. He was 82. He left the store to his employees, "really fine people."

For updates on O'Hurley's, "purveyor of time-tested merchandise," visit the Facebook page.

Along the Way: Eye of Shepherdstown

"By odds the most remarkable thing in Shepherdstown is a wooden eye a foot long. It rests on a Bible; also of wood and is inserted in the wall of a little bit of a market-house, over which is an Odd-Fellows Hall. The 'all-seeing eye' was never more boldly treated. You must go see it."

GEORGE W. BAGBY, 1881

Bagby's words remain as true today as they were when he penned them—the old market-house building in Shepherdstown, is still must-see attraction.

The two-story, narrow structure stands in the middle of King Street, although its address is 100 German Street. Flanked by alleys, the building's odd siting is the result of its original use as a one-story market house. It was built in 1800, a single-story structure measuring 57 by 20 feet.

The spot was the heart of both commerce and restitution. A whipping post and public hog pen were on the building's south side. Persons found guilty of violating town ordinances were punished here, and a hog found running loose in the community was rounded up, placed in the pen, and sold at auction.

In keeping with its function, the building had open construction with stalls on the sides facing King Street. Wooden slats covered the stall openings when the market was closed. Large doors were at each end of the building.

In 1845 the Shepherdstown Town Council granted a 999-year lease to the International Order of Odd Fellows, which added a second story to

The former IOOF Hall in Shepherdstown stands in the middle of King Street.

the building for a meeting hall. Nine years later, the town market closed; the first floor was renovated to create a firehouse. The stalls were enclosed with brick exterior walls, thus setting the stage for a string of future uses: council chambers, private school, and meat market.

In the aftermath of the Battle of Antietam in nearby Maryland, September 17, 1862, the building was pressed into service as a makeshift hospital for wounded soldiers. By the early 1920s, only a couple of jail stalls remained as the prior tenants upgraded to better quarters elsewhere. Shepherdstown citizens called for the building's demolition. But that 999-year lease was a problem; it blocked demolition just as the building itself seemed to block traffic on King Street.

The Shepherdstown Women's Club, in 1926, obtained the town council's permission to use the building as a public library. Jail cells continued to occupy it until 1948, when they were removed to free up space for the library. The Odd Fellows in 1962 agreed to sell the remainder of its second-floor lease to the women's club. The club continued to operate the library until 1971, when it relinquished the asset to the West Virginia Library Commission. With that move, The Shepherdstown Library expanded into the balance of the structure, except for a kitchen that the women's club retained. More remodeling occurred, but its tenants were careful to preserve the historical remnants from its IOOF days, including the all-seeing eye.

Eventually, the historic structure's inadequacies became too much for a 21st century information hub, and a new library was built at 145 Higbee Street. The library relocated in the summer 2022. Town council is reviewing options for the eye building in the heart of Shepherdstown.

Chapter 2

The Iron Man

Seventy-two-year-old Bryan Richard "Jim" Davis cleared the tools and tires away from his set of fitness weights, stiffened in front of the bar, and squarely placed his hands thereupon. He took a deep breath, and with every muscle in his body working in unison, raised the 500-pound set of weights above the stand for a few agonizing seconds.

Grinning at his accomplishment, Jim picked up a 50-pound block of metal, walked outdoors and swung it above his head. He concluded this demonstration of senior strength by grabbing a vertical metal pole with his bare hands and pulling himself perpendicular to the pole, flapping in the Harrison County breeze like a human flag wearing a "JESUS SAVES" baseball cap.

"Whatever a person does, I think before you can do anything, you got to ask for God's help," Jim told me.

The night he "broke his back" is a good example. He was employed as a welder at a remote coalmine site and was the last person there as it closed for the weekend. As he packed up his welding equipment, he discovered that

Jim Davis uses a pole in his yard to demonstrate his strength at the age of 73. Photo from April 2006

his welding leads were pinned under the tires of his two-ton truck. Rather than move the vehicle, Jim tried to free the leads with his sheer strength.

"I put the welding lead down the middle of my back, squatted down and pulled as hard as I could," he said. "When I raised up, I proceeded to break my back. I pulled that lead out and broke my back."

Jim was numb from the waist down and couldn't walk.

"I knew what I had done is cram them backbones together, them knuckles in the sockets, too tightly. I had asked too much of my bones, and they popped out of their sockets. When they jumped out, they pinched my spinal cord right there," Jim told me, pointing to the affected area.

He had no radio, no cell phone, and it would be 60 hours before the next crew reported for work.

"I didn't lay there very long," he said. "The very first thing I did is pray. I looked up and said, 'Lord, I'm in a bind. Are you going to let me crawl around like a snake for the rest of my life for being stupid?'"

It was déjà vu for the strong man whose strength often got him in as

The stair rails provided another opportunity for Jim to demonstrate his strength.

many binds as it rescued him from. Back in the 1950s, while returning to his car from hunting, Jim jumped off a 100-foot-high wall of rock (no explanation for why). Praying all the way down, Jim raised his shotgun above his head with both hands. The elevated weapon broke his fall as he dropped into a pile of brush.

God and common sense helped him get out of the "broken back" dilemma, as well. He devised a risky solution based upon prior observation: Doctors use traction to restore compressed vertebrae to their proper locations. Jim decided to use materials at hand to accomplish a similar effect.

Using his immense upper-body strength, he pulled himself to the toolbox on the back of his truck and wrapped a length of chain around his ankles. He secured the ends of the chain to his toolbox.

"I made sure I had just about what I needed for a hangman's job," he said of the chain. "I wanted that jerk when I got to the end."

Jim flipped the toolbox off the truck and braced himself for the jerk. The effect was immediate.

"Praise the Lord," he said. "I felt my legs again. When I got back on my feet, I could hardly stand up. It felt like I was walking on pins and needles, like they were gouging me all over. But, you know, sometimes pain is a good feeling. Whenever you have no feeling, pain is a good feeling."

Jim drove himself home, and when he walked in the door that night, told his wife, Virginia, "I'm a walking miracle."

He never received a proper medical evaluation, but more than 20 years after he administered hillbilly traction, Jim Davis was still doing incredible things with his back.

Sculpting his yard

He lived on Cunningham Run, northwest of Shinnston. Arriving there on an April afternoon in 2006, I knew from the initial contact I'd found the right house in this isolated valley when I spotted a driveway lined with metal flowers "blooming" against a landscape still recovering from winter. Most of these welded sculptures measured 3 to 4 feet across and rested on stems of 4-inch chain with welded links. Sheet metal and hot water tanks contributed the metal for the petals and leaves.

The largest of these creations, a sunflower, was 25 feet above the sloping yard and required a crane to erect. As fearless of heights as he was of administering toolbox traction, Jim shimmied up the pole, took a perch on a seat behind the flower, and stretched out his arms for my camera.

"Look Ma, no hands!" Jim declared.

Back on the ground, Jim told me that the pipe supporting the sunflower came from a gas line that once crossed his property." They were removing (the line), and I said, 'How about saving me a couple joints of that?'" Jim said.

Most of the ornaments on his lawn and much of the furniture in his house resulted from this penchant for recycling and Jim's occupation as a welder. Working at coal mines gave him access to a variety of scrap metal, from the large teeth of loading buckets to road grader exhausts; from suspension springs to bulldozer bearing hubs.

The latter served as sunflower pistils. For a morning glory's light-blue, trumpet-shaped blossom, Jim re-purposed agitators from washing machines. A discarded piece of sheet metal provided stock for day lily blooms.

Jim Davis and his wife, Virginia Mae, with one of his scrap-metal sunflowers.

"When I got done with that one, I said to my wife, 'See that bunch of flowers over there? Well, this bud's for you!'" Jim said with a big smile, referring to the brewery's slogan.

The bigger-than-life trillium, Jack-in-the-pulpit, holly bush, turkey, and blue heron in his yard shared a common ferrous ancestry—a stash of scrap metal enclosed by a fence in Jim's yard.

Charlie the Miner was commissioned by Phil Southern of Repair King in Shinnston as a memorial to his coal miner father and others who died mining coal. Jim Davis made the sculpture from discarded water heaters.

"I'd get exhaust systems from big old dozers, trucks, backhoes. Any time we would dismantle something, I'd carry the scrap away. That kind of pleased them (at the mines) because I'd go around and gather up the junk," Jim said.

Jim stockpiled the discards thinking he would eventually sell them when the value of scrap metal rose. The prices languished, however, and Jim turned to making lawn ornaments and furniture from the castoffs.

His work received recognition, and he was commissioned to make a 22-foot-tall miner for Coal Country Miniature Golf Course in Fairmont. That led to a second commission, an 18-foot-tall miner for Repair King, a mining-equipment repair company in Shinnston.

Phil Southern, Repair King owner, told me that he commissioned the piece as a memorial to his father, who lost his life in a Kansas coalmine disaster in 1951. The statue is named "Charlie the Miner."

"I saw the (first) one he'd made, and I thought that would be a nice thing for us to do," Phil said.

Phil paid $14,000 for the sculpture fashioned from discarded hot water heaters. A crane was required to erect it at the company's Lincoln Center headquarters. Dedicated in 1999, it stands as the centerpiece of a brick plaza dedicated as a memorial to all miners who died working the coal industry.

Jim created the sculpture from a concept drawing; a soda delivery truck driver who happened to be in the room while Jim and Phil discussed the project provided the proportions.

"I measured a guy who came to restock the Coke machine," Jim said. "He was 2 feet across at the shoulders and 6 feet, 2 inches. I made everything 3:1 on that coal miner, so he's 18 feet, 6 inches tall and 6 feet wide at the shoulders."

Jim applied a fresh coat of paint to the nameless memorial each year.

"I climb a ladder and paint that guy," he said. "The last time I painted him, the paint was too light in color, and it looked like the guy had poison ivy and they'd put calamine lotion all over him."

A personal financial crunch sent Jim in a new direction sometime after he completed the miner sculpture. "I ran out of oxygen and acetylene," he said. "I thought I'd see if I can make something out of wood. I said, 'God, here's a piece of wood, I'd like you to make something out of it.'"

That something turned out to be a bald eagle clutching a trout with its talons. Many more carvings followed: the West Virginia state seal, a dark coon-hunting scene inspired by his childhood experiences in the woods, a smaller eagle flag-holder, and a deacon's bench with morning-glory motifs.

"While I was carving that, a bird came into the garage and tried to get in one of those flowers. I said, 'Thank you, Lord.' That was a real compliment," Jim said.

He transformed a cherry log into his largest carving, another bald eagle. It had a wingspan of 76 inches and was unfinished at the time of my visit. Jim said he'd have to sell it once it was completed; it was too large for his home.

Jim Davis made his tools for carving large pieces like this eagle from logs.

"I don't know of anybody who'd want to put that in their house, but I'd like to sell it," he said.

Jim made many of his carving tools for these projects. He adapted a broken electric chisel to pneumatic power, then fabricated a variety of attachments for chiseling out the carving's details.

One of his most challenging carvings was a lamp and its shade fashioned from the trunk of a cherry tree surrounded by a grapevine. The tree followed the vine's twisted course for several feet before breaking free and growing straight again.

"That was fascinating to me. That was a remarkable piece of wood . . . something God did. What fascinates me is how God made that join back together at the top," he said, studying the lamp.

Jim removed the bark and vine from the tree trunk to reveal the spiral. He created the lampshade from a maple log. He sawed off a 1-inch-thick section of the log for the lamp base, then hollowed out the remaining section of log to leave behind just the bark and a thin layer of the substrate.

"I used chisels and drills," he said. "I'd drill holes and then cut across them. It took me a couple of weeks to get that cleaned out."

Jim Davis prayed about each project that he tackled, including making this lamp from a section of a tree that a grape vine had wrapped itself around. He used the lamp as an object lesson when he spoke to groups about drug addiction and finding God.

Jim found a spiritual use for the lamp; he took it to Sunday school classes and used it as an object lesson in how God repairs a believer's life with divine chisels.

"I tell them drugs can put a squeeze on their lives, that drugs can tear you apart, but if you turn your life over to God, he will cause your life to come back together," he said.

Jim expressed his faith and talents by performing hymns on his harmonica and guitar and singing with his wife. He wrote many of the songs they sang, verses that reflected his faith in God and fascination with the natural world. Whatever project he tackled, Jim asked for divine direction before picking up his chisel, welding rod, or pen.

Lifting weights in the barn

Credit also went to the isolated, rural childhood he knew while growing up on the family dairy farm in nearby Flatwoods, Braxton County. Jim was born in a log cabin to Lava and Lona Gregory Davis. His given name is Bryan Richard, but his family called him "Jim" because he had wrinkled skin as a baby.

"My mom and dad lived beside an old fella, Jim. He was wrinkled up like a prune. I had wrinkled skin, so they called me 'Old Jim.' Well, I got quite a few wrinkles now, and I tell people that when you got wrinkles, that's just room to stretch."

And stretch he did. Jim became interested in weightlifting when he was 16. "One night my uncle was showing off—he could hold an anvil in his hand on an outstretched arm. He influenced me to exercise. I was doing 75 push-ups every night before I went to bed," Jim told me.

He built up his muscles to the point he could eventually lift a 100-pound bag of dairy feed with one arm and raise it above his head. He converted a portion of a loft in the family's dairy barn to a gymnasium. "When a guy is out in the country, he learns to entertain himself," Jim said.

He followed a vocational path in high school, learning welding, machine trades, and typing. "That way, if I got out of work, I was so well-rounded that if they needed something typed, I could type it for them, then I could go out and fix their machinery."

In the early 1950s Jim put those typing skills to work in the Navy, where he was a supply clerk. After serving his country, Jim went back to the family farm, then tried coal mining. When his brother narrowly escaped death in the Farmington Mine explosion, Jim headed to northeast Ohio, where he worked as a construction laborer and trained as a miner.

He and Virginia Mae Hall were married by then. The couple eloped under the pretense of going to a drive-in movie; they went to Weston, instead, and found a pastor to marry them. They honeymooned at the home of Jim's grandparents, but Jim's reputation as a joker almost spoiled the night. His grandfather refused to allow Virginia Mae to enter his home as a bride without proper documentation. The customary events continued to unfold only after Jim returned to the car and produced the license.

Jim and Virginia had two boys and three girls. After several years in

Jim Davis with a few of his scrap-metal creations, April 2007.

Ohio, they returned to West Virginia, where he purchased their home near Peora in 1970. "The coal mines in West Virginia were paying higher than they were in Ohio," he said.

He found even better wages and consistent employment as a contract welder. "I made more money that way than I made in the coal mines," he said. Good training and enjoying the work ensured success for him.

"If a person does what he likes to do, you'll do a better job on every job you do. If you enjoy your work, you'll look forward to getting out of bed every day," he said.

As with everything else in Jim's life, his faith played a role in that success.

"I live by John 3:27. A man can receive only what is given him from heaven,'" Jim said. "I believe if a man wants something, he's got to ask God."

Jim also applied that to his pastime of riding motorcycles. He owned a dozen or so in his lifetime, starting with a 1941 Indian Chief he purchased from his older brother, Harold, while working in Ohio. He and Virginia were the owners of a 1977 Kawasaki when I visited him. They used it in the Bikers for Christ ministry.

"God has a sense of humor," he said. "I was praying for a Harley Davidson,

Jim Davis hangs from a 25-foot pole in his yard as he inspects his tallest sculpture, a sunflower. Jim seemed to have no fear of heights.

and he gave me one of those old Japanese bikes. It's the craziest thing I ever seen. It's got too much power for my wife. She thinks it's a racing bike."

Before leaving that day, Jim pulled out his harmonica and played one of his tunes for me. He explained how he came to master the instrument, one more tool in this talented man's life-saving toolbox. Jim said one of his uncles owned and played harmonicas, and one of the instruments came into his possession. His irritating efforts to coax music from the mouth organ resulted in an ultimatum.

"Mom was going to throw the thing away," he said. "She said, 'If you don't learn to play that thing right, it won't be here when you get up in the morning.'"

Jim Davis wrote and performed many gospel songs; the harmonica was one of the instruments he could play. He also was one of the nicest persons I've ever met in West Virginia.

Jim took out the hymnal, turned to "He Hideth My Soul," and played the song perfectly.

"She said, 'The harmonica is yours,'" Jim recalled.

Bryan Richard "Jim" Davis died September 25, 2021, at the age of 88. Virginia died the following year.

Carl and Shirley Yokum stand inside one of the tepees he built as part of their Princess Snowbird Campground at Seneca Rocks. The couple developed and operated many of the tourist-services business at the popular destination. Photo from October 2007.

Chapter 3

Yokum's Vacation Land

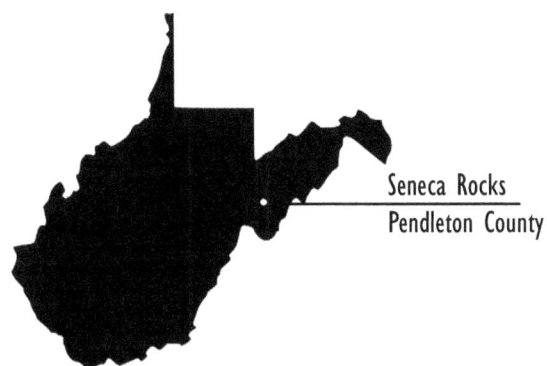

Seneca Rocks
Pendleton County

Looming 900 feet above the valley, Seneca Rocks is one of West Virginia's iconic natural wonders. The rocks are located at the intersection of West Virginia routes 33 and 55 and are contained within the Monongahela National Forest, Spruce Knob-Seneca Rocks Recreation Area. The North Fork of the South Branch of the Potomac and Seneca Creek merge near the rocks.

The rocks are on the west flank of the Willis Mountain Anticline, a geologic stratum that more than 200 million years ago was upended and rotated 90 degrees. They are made of Tuscarora quartzite (sandstone) that was deposited when the waters of an ancient sea covered what is now West Virginia. As one travels south on Route 33 from Seneca Rocks to Judy Gap, other Tuscarora formations appear on the high ridges.

For the adventurous, the sheer faces of these outcroppings are challenges to be subdue with ropes, strength, and mental focus. One moment of distraction can result in death. But scaling the rocks for recreation is a relatively recent development. When Paul Bradt, Don Hubbard, and Sam Moore ascended the rocks in 1939, they discovered an inscription, "D. B. (or

Towering 900 feet above the valley, Scenca Rocks is a breathtaking feature that draws many rock climbers to it challenging face. For the less adventurous, a walking trail on the back side of the rocks reaches the top, as well.

possibly H.) September 16, 1908." If the second letter is a "B," the intrepid explorer was probably a surveyor, Donald Bittenger. If it is an "H," D.C. Harper, whose family owned the rocks, was likely the adventurer.

World War II and the Allies' planned invasion of Italy, which would require scaling the Apennines, thrust the rocks into a national security role. Soldiers from the 10th Mountain Division of the U.S. Army used Seneca, Nelson, and Champe rocks as training grounds for alpine-warfare skills. Known as The West Virginia Maneuver Area, this training operation invaded the Seneca Rocks area and Blackwater Canyon in 1943 and 1944.

With the rocks a known habitat for rattlesnakes, legends of soldiers being bitten or lowered into dens of the poisonous reptiles emerged from the months of training exercises. My maternal grandparents shared these tales with me when they took me to the rocks as a child. Researchers, however, have found no documentation to support these legends. Snakes aside, hazards abounded from equipment failure to a misplaced foot while scaling the ice-covered rocks in winter.

Falling rocks kill most of the climbers who have tackled the face since those WWII soldiers left behind some 75,000 soft-steel pinons in the formation. Although exact statistics were unavailable, more than a dozen

US soldiers trained in mountain climbing on Seneca Rocks to prepare them for scaling the Apennines during the Allied invasion of Italy. *Acme News Photos, West Virginia and Regional History Center at WVU.*

climbers have died on these since 1971. Causes include falls, being pelted with rocks from above, heart attacks, and exposure. Still undaunted? There are at least 375 identified paths to the top!

Fortunately, you can get a sweeping view of the valley from the top of the rocks and not risk your life in the process. A path up the backside makes this possible, but it is an arduous hike and should not be attempted

The 25-foot tall Gendarme that stood in the formation's "gun sight" toppled October 22, 1987.

if you lack physical conditioning/appropriate footwear or have medical issues. I walked it many years ago, and it took about 45 minutes. Neither my wife nor my cardiologist would approve of a repeat visit at the age of 70.

Seneca Rocks takes it name from the Seneca Indian tribe, one of the six tribes in the Iroquois Federation. The Senecas are said to have wintered in the limestone caves of this region. Perhaps these long winters underground inspired them to spin a few legends around the smoky fires. The one about Princess Snowbird is the most famous.

She was the beautiful and only daughter of Chief Bald Eagle and his wife, White Rock. Snowbird grew up in the shadow of the rocks and, as a young girl, mastered the path to the pinnacle. Thus, when it came time to choose a mate from the seven warrior suitors, she devised a test of bravery and determination: She would make her assent, and the first warrior to reach her would win her hand in marriage.

Some of the men turned back out of fear, others faltered along the climb. Only one came within an arm's length of the princess, and then he began to fall. Seeing his bravery, Snowbird reached out her hand and rescued him. They were married and, of course, lived happily ever after.

Like many legends, there is probably a grain of truth in the story. Indeed,

The view from the overlook at Seneca Rocks is worth the strenuous climb up the rocks' backside.

a blog post about it solicited a response from a reader who claimed to be the reincarnation of the man who Snowbird married. Further, he claimed that his wife was the reincarnation of Snowbird, and that their happiness was short lived because of the fighting between competing tribes. They knew the only way to end the fighting was for them to return to the pinnacle and jump off.[1]

Another legend connected to the rocks was that Snowbird waited for her suitors in the notch, or "gun sight," of the formation. A 25-foot-tall freestanding pinnacle, or Gendarme, stood in this notch and supposedly represented the maiden, although the feature was likely there for 440 million years before the legend was spun. The Gendarme fell from its perch 3:27 p.m. October 22, 1987.[2] Most experts agreed that its demise was due to natural causes and old age.

1   Mountainword, Words From The Mountains: The Legend of Princess Snowbird, accessed January 22, 2024 https://wordsfromthemountains.blogspot.com/2009/05/legend-of-princess-snowbird.html

2   Donald P. Baker, Famed W.Va. Rock Takes Tumble after 440 Million Years, The Washington Post, accessed January 22, 2024 https://www.washingtonpost.com/archive/local/1987/10/29/famed-wva-rock-takes-tumble-after-440-million-years/29f5d8fc-4598-4110-8cba-b9f188a41dc6/

Carl and Shirley Yokum were married during the Great Depression. They went to grade school together and both were from families who had been in the Mouth of Seneca area for generations. *Yokum family collection.*

Love in hard times

Carl and Shirley Yokum didn't have a dramatic love story like that associated with the Native American lore of Seneca Rocks. But their seven decades of marriage and incessant labor in the shadow of this magnificent formation made for a Pendleton County hospitality legend—Yokum's Vacationland.

The enterprise included their store and motel at the busy intersection of routes 55 and 33. Just across Seneca Creek was their Princess Snowbird's Campground and Indian Village, which had primitive camping, honeymoon cabins, and tepees.

Traveling northeast toward Petersburg on Route 33, the tourist encountered more of this hospitality dynasty: a restaurant, a second motel, five modern log cabins, and a second campground. Carl and Shirley also owned the old school where they studied as youngsters, the modern Seneca Rocks

The Sites family homestead at Seneca Rocks, 1984. Jacob Sites settled at the rocks in 1839. A reproduction of his home stands near a visitors' parking lot. *Photo from the West Virginia and Regional History Center at West Virginia University.*

Elementary building, their home, and several other houses. They even owned the land that included the family cemetery—and still more.

Across the private bridge that spanned the North Fork of the South Branch of the Potomac River was the Yokum cattle farm and original homestead, the homes of Yokum grandchildren, and riding stables that offered horseback rides to the top of the rocks. Carl also owned pasture lands elsewhere in the region. Except for the stables, these properties were operated by Carl, who was in his early 90s, and Shirley, in her late 80s, when I visited them in 2006.

Both Shirley's and Carl's families went back several generations in their connections to this land. Shirley (Bland) traced her ancestry to Jacob Sites, who settled at the rocks in 1839. A reconstruction of his pioneer site built by the U.S. Department of the Interior stands near a parking lot at the rocks. His descendants owned the famous rocks before the U.S. Government condemned the property in the 1960s in an action that left deep resentment among those whose ancestral heritage was snatched from them for a fraction of its true value.

Jacob Sites' original holdings were divided among children in successive

Farming was in Carl Yokum's genes. In addition to building and maintaining Vacationland properties, Carl managed and feed hundreds of cattle on his land around the rocks.

generations. Shirley's maternal grandmother, Delzena "Della," inherited the land on which Yokum's store stands. Her parents and grandfather started the store.

The Yokum connection to the land northeast of the Mouth of Seneca goes back to the late 1860s, when Adam Yokum married Rebecca Mouse, whose father had a farm in this valley. Adam served in Company I, 7th regiment of the West Virginia Volunteer Infantry. He fought at Antietam, Gettysburg, Chancellorsville, and the Second Battle of Bull Run. Adam lived to be 84 and shared many of his Civil War tales with his 14 grandchildren, Carl being one of them.

The son of Esten and Elizabeth (Judy) Yokum, Carl's family had a history of both agriculture and hospitality by living on the cattle-drive route that extended from Virginia to the Sinks of Gandy, a popular summer grazing area. A cattle drive between Moorefield and the sinks typically required three days, and the Mouth of Seneca was a popular place to overnight. The Yokums had both the pasture and rooms to accommodate livestock and

Yokums' Princess Snowbird Indian Village and Campground, seen from near the peak of Seneca Rocks, sprawls over the valley. It was one of several hospitality businesses the couple built and operated.

their drovers as they passed through the gap. Carl shared stories of these common sights from his childhood.

"This one guy would drive 50 head of cattle out of here himself and a big collie dog, and they would stay over here at my home across the river," Carl recalled. "We had a pen across here, this place above the road, they could turn them in there for the night.

"This old dog, many times when they'd be coming down here by the river, he'd get ahead of those cattle and stop them at that gate. And as soon as they put them in, he'd head across this old bridge and he'd go to the kitchen door (of the Yokum home) and he'd bark, and my mother would come out and put them up for the night. His name was Tom Ford, Tom Ford was the guy that drove them. He'd have to stay at about three different places along the way. He worked for a big farmer in Moorefield."

Tourists arrive

When the highway between Seneca Rocks and Petersburg was paved in the mid-1930s, Carl sensed impending opportunity. Dating back to the

Carl and Shirley Yokum in front of their beloved Seneca Rocks.

Seneca Indians, this area had a reputation for fine hunting and fishing. Carl liked to fish and knew there were plenty of bass what would attract a strong tourist trade once the valley became accessible to motorists.

Carl constructed the two seminal cabins of what would become Yokum's Vacationland on the flat land between the highway and the North Fork. Built of green logs that Carl felled and hewed, the cabins lasted 50 years. His mother helped him cover the interior walls with cheesecloth, which provided a base for wallpaper. Each cabin had only a bed and washstand; a nearby well topped off with a hand pump provided the "running water." He figured he had about $25 to $30 invested in each cabin.

"I built two and rented them for a dollar a night, $5 a week. That's when a dollar was worth a dollar," Carl said. "My first customers were two guys from Ohio. They came in here and they paid me a dollar for one day. They cooked fish and everything, and they wanted to stay the rest of the week, so they paid me $4. When they got to the end of the week, they wanted to know if they could stay another week. When they got to leave, they said they were a bit short on money and wanted to know if I'd take their check, but it bounced. So, I got $5 for the first two weeks I was in business."

With the family farm and a fledgling tourist business to offer, Carl asked Shirley to be his wife. Shirley and Carl met as grade-school students in

The Yokums "lived off the land" while building their Vacationland. Carl caught the ugly hellgrammites that lived in the streams around Seneca Rocks and sold them to fishermen for 40 cents a dozen.

the little schoolhouse they own. "In elementary school, we used to write letters back and forth," Shirley recalled.

After graduating from Circleville High School, Shirley went to Akron, Ohio, where she stayed with her aunt while attending business school. Akron and its huge tire industry was a landing ground for Appalachian migrants in search of a better life. Shirley's desire was to be a nurse, and she earned a scholarship to that end. Her family didn't have the cash to match her grant, and she chose business school, instead.

Carl stayed behind, farmed, and added to the infrastructure of his tourist-services venture. They were married in Winchester, Virginia, October 7, 1938.

"We had this minister from a Presbyterian church who came around here, and he told us whenever we got married, he wanted to be the one to marry us," Shirley said. "So, we went down to Winchester where he lived and got married and went on to Washington (D.C.) for our honeymoon."

Carl's cabin holdings had grown to four by 1938, but the couple stayed in the Yokum farmhouse until Carl had built a proper house for them. He harvested logs from the farm with a crosscut saw; his father's cousin helped him mill those oak and pine logs into 20,000 board feet of lumber, which was dried in a kiln Carl built. They moved into the new house in 1940, and Shirley promptly opened a tourist home.

"My mother always kept a couple of boarders," Shirley said, explaining the inspiration for her business. "They would be working on the road or whatever, and there was no place for them to stay. She did that from the time I was a little kid. So that's where I got that from."

Within three years, the couple had two children plus cabins, a tourist home that served meals, and a farm.

"It wasn't easy," said Shirley, who charged 30 cents for a home-cooked meal. To make extra money, they caught hellgrammites (larvae of the Dobson fly) in the river and sold them to fishermen at 40 cents a dozen.

"We did whatever we could to make money," Shirley said. "He'd catch animals and skin them, dry the hides and sell those. We bought the paint for our house with the money from that. We worked hard, believe me."

The soldiers arrive

World War II brought gas rationing, which decreased the tourist trade. Soldiers eventually replaced tourists when Seneca Rocks became the site of the military training school for rock climbing. The Yokum Tourist Home accommodated the camp doctors, instructors, visiting officers and, occasionally, their wives. "We even had a lieutenant and his wife sleep in our kitchen," Shirley recalled.

"Carl used to cut hair for the soldiers in our basement," Shirley said. "They'd give him a quarter to do that. He asked me to cut his hair one time; it was the last time he ever did that."

On Saturday nights, the couple provided soldiers with transportation to the movie theater in Petersburg. Carl put benches in the bed of their truck and hauled the men to town in that. "They would sing all the way down the road," Shirley said.

During one of those trips, the truck's headlights failed, and Carl had to drive the twisting road in darkness. Because there was a canvas cover over the truck bed and the men were preoccupied with singing, they never knew Carl was navigating by starlight and his familiarity with the route.

Steady growth marked the post-war years for both their business and the region. Columbia Gas brought a distribution line across the mountain

For many years after they built their restaurant at Seneca Rocks, Shirley Yokum worked as the cook. It had a reputation for the fine Sunday dinner buffet featuring several gourmet dishes that she learned to prepare at the Greenbrier Cooking School.

and built a pumping station just north of their home. Carl helped build it and was hired as an operator. For 29 years, he balanced the full-time job with farming and myriad vacationland responsibilities, which included constructing a new cabin every year.

Carl also served as a fire warden for 45 years, leading a crew of six to eight firefighters. During the WWII years, forest fires were frequent in the region, as a consequence of the war maneuvers and military presence. He said the worst fire he ever fought was on Dolly Sods, the site of an artillery range from October 1943 to the summer of 1944 (an unexploded shell is occasionally discovered by a hiker or camper). The fire raged for three days and three nights, and 1,000 acres burned.

In 1947, the couple built the restaurant. "I bought that old garage building up there. It was a CCC camp, it was all good lumber. That's what I built that out of," Carl said.

Shirley was the restaurant's cook for many years and went to the Greenbrier Cooking School to improve her skills. During the 1950s, the restaurant served a Sunday buffet of all homemade items that usually included one or two gourmet dishes. The perennial favorite, however, was their sausage made from hogs raised on the Yokum farm.

Shirley Yokum handled the reservations for Yokum's hospitality businesses, assisted in the restaurant, did the bookkeeping duties, and kept up with trends in the tourism industry. She also managed Yokum's Store, which once belonged to her mother, and volunteered as an EMT..

"We used to make our own sausage, brown it in the oven, and can it," she said. "They'd come from miles around just to get some of my sausage."

Not content with a tourist home, cabins, and restaurant, the couple purchased Yokum's Store from Shirley's mother when she was ready to retire. They expanded it to include a motel with kitchenette rooms and built two campgrounds and a second motel. Carl said they constantly re-invested their profits in the business.

"Lots of times we spent the last 50-cent piece we had, and we didn't know where the next one was coming from," Carl said.

Shirley was the entrepreneur, always looking for a new opportunity amid the challenges. The couple kept riding horses about an hour's drive

Shirley Yokum trained as an Emergency Medical Technician and served on the Grant County Ambulance crews that responded to emergencies in the popular recreational area of Seneca Rocks.

from their home, "and we had to drive over there every weekend, and we had to hire a man to stay over and take care of the horses," Shirley said. "We rode up in the woods and you rode back and couldn't see anything. We owned the whole side of this rock, back up in this holler, all the way up. I just got another brainstorm one day, and I hired a man with a 14-foot-wide blade (on his bulldozer), and I said, 'You follow me and we're going to build this trail.'"

Thus began the horse-riding trail to Seneca Rocks, another Yokum enterprise. In the hands of their grandson Virgil "Bub" Yokum, Seneca Rocks Stables made three trips a day to the top of the rocks. The trail was wide enough for emergency vehicles and thus provided a lifesaving resource for the many climbers, as well. Indeed, Shirley's interest in the welfare of her neighbors led to her becoming an emergency medical technician. She served as EMT on the Grant County Ambulance crew for 10 years, her way of fulfilling that adolescent dream of becoming a nurse.

With so many irons in the fire, maintaining a marriage could have been a challenge. But they respected each other's dreams and always made time for each other.

Carl Yokum stands in the doorway of one of the tepees at the Yokums' Princess Snowbird Indian Village and Campground. The couple got the idea for the unusual accommodation while traveling in the western states.

"He learned to let me do my own thing," Shirley told me. "And whenever we got too bogged down, I'd take him on a long trip. You have to keep him interested."

They traveled to every state except North Dakota and visited Ireland, Cuba, Jamaica, China, Australia, and the Middle East. Carl climbed Ayer's Rock in Australia at the age of 80. Shirley earned a tour guide certificate from the North American School of Travel. Their trips were often working vacations as Shirley researched hospitality trends and attractions in other regions.

"I would see something and come home and try it," Shirley said. That's how her "brainstorm" of building tepees in the Princess Snowbird Campground came about. The tepees were 12-feet in diameter at the base, a concrete slab. The frames were long poles of an extremely hard wood from North Dakota. Originally, canvas was spread over these frames and decorated in Native-American motifs. "Some hoodlums went in there one night and slit every one of them," Shirley said. "I lost them all."

Undaunted, Carl and Shirley rebuilt five of the twelve original tepees, this time using aluminum flashing on the exterior and silver-backed insulation board for the wall. The floors were tiled for easy maintenance.

A small, simple wood door that required adults to duck before entering and a single window were the only openings in the tepees. Despite the relative lack of ventilation, their interiors stayed cool, thanks to the insulation and a ceiling fan. The Yokums rented them throughout the year; a portable electric heater took the edge off the cold Pendleton County nights.

Amid all the responsibilities and hard work of building and running their businesses, the couple found time to raise their four children: Jack, Sharon (Maluo), Patsy (White), and Sam. Shirley said their youngsters grew up working in the business with the understanding their parents would put them through college on one condition: they didn't think about marriage until after they'd earned their degrees. "They knew better to even ask," Shirley said.

Over the years, their family also included 15 foster children.

"I'm always looking for a challenge," Shirley told me. "And believe me, I've had a lot of them in my life."

The most significant came in 1985, when flooding on the North Fork wiped out the original campground and reduced the cabins, including those dating from the 1930s, to flotsam. Carl also lost his farming equipment to the floodwaters. Their total monetary losses were around a half-million dollars, and they were uninsured.

Even worse was the loss of life. Stelman and Harry Harper, Shirley's uncles, died in the flood as they returned from delivering cattle to Petersburg.

Both Shirley and Carl were beyond normal "retirement age" when the flood came, but they rebuilt Vacationland. This time, Carl built his cabins on higher ground.

"There is no point in giving up," Shirley said. "You just keep going. I have this thing that pushes me. I have to have something going on all the time."

While Carl and Shirley employed more than a dozen people to help them run Vacationland, they remained hands-on operators who were on call 24 hours a day.

Carl maintained the properties and grounds and oversaw his herd of up to 400 cattle. Shirley took reservations, kept the books, and was often in the restaurant during the day. The creative spark of the business, she was always looking for new opportunities and ideas, like hanging a clear plastic bag full of water above the restaurant entrance.

"It keeps the flies out," Shirley said. "They see their reflection in there and they think it's a spider." Strange as it sounds, Shirley insisted it works. "Everything that works is fine with me," she said.

She was always looking for the next opportunity that would capitalize on the rocks' mesmerizing majesty.

"I've often thought they should have an elevator put up there to take people to the top of the rocks," Shirley said.

The magnificent Tuscarora sandstone formation inspired the creative thinking and the hard work epitomized in Carl and Shirley Yokum.

"When we travel and come back, I say we have more to see here than anyplace else," she said.

Carl Yokum died at his home on November 5, 2008. He was 92.

Shirley Yokum lived to be 100 and passed August 8, 2020, at Grant Rehabilitation and Care Center, Petersburg. She was the recipient of the Lifetime Achievement Award from the Pendleton County Chamber of Commerce and considered to be one of the most formidable and accomplished businesswomen of eastern West Virginia.

Chapter 4

Harper's Store

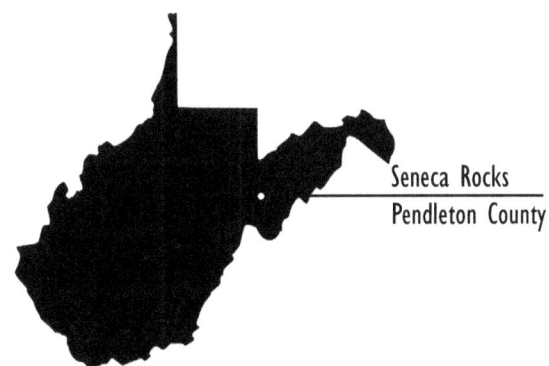
Seneca Rocks
Pendleton County

In an age when most small towns have seen their general stores go the way of 32-cent-a-gallon gasoline, Seneca Rocks, the crossroads in the shadow of the namesake formation, is an anomaly.

The town, once known as Mouth of Seneca, has two general stores with only a driveway separating them. The coziness is more than coincidental; the store's namesake owners trace their ancestries to Jacob Sites, who settled in this valley in 1839.

Jacob's land was divided and subdivided among his descendants with each generation. His granddaughters, Anna and Delzena "Della" Sites, ended up with the two parcels that host the general stores; Anna, who married Joseph Martin Harper, got the parcel to the north; Della, who married Stewart L. Bland, got the other one.

Their husbands went into shopkeeping: Harper in 1902, Bland in 1923.

Bland's Store, now Yokum's, was built by Shirley Yokum's parents, Byron and Erma (Harper) Bland, and Byron's father, Stewart. Bryon was a World War I veteran, teacher, mail carrier, and shopkeeper. Erma Bland was a

Yokum's Store at Seneca Rocks catered to the camper and outdoor enthusiast who needed quick refreshment and basic supplies. It shares the same intersection with Harper's at Seneca Rocks.

self-taught medicine woman who drew her supplies from the mountains and knowledge from tradition and necessity.

"People would come in from up and down the mountain asking, 'What can you do for this or that?'" Shirley Yokum told me back in 2007. "Our mother could mix her own salve. She made her own gargle. You won't find a better gargle," said Shirley, who took over the store when her mother retired.

The gargle concoction contained vinegar, soda, salt, powered alum, and water. "It fizzles, it doesn't matter, you gargle with it and it will stop a sore throat," Shirley said.

Shirley and her husband Carl modernized their store, Yokum's General, and transformed its second story into a motel with a front-porch view of the famed rocks. With a bright interior, the walls lined with beverage coolers and the long rows of steel shelving devoted to groceries, snacks, and souvenirs, it looked like a typical suburban convenience store.

Joe and Carolyn Harper, fourth-generation owners of Harper's General Store, took an entirely different approach to their store. "We want to be a step back," Joe told me during a visit in May 2008.

Established in 1902 by Joe's great grandfather, J. M. Harper, Harper's

J.M. Harper and carpenters named the "Cooks from Circleville" built Harper's Store at Seneca Rocks in 1902. Circa 1912, Harper's son, D.C., took over the store. D.C.'s son "Buck" bought it in 1969, and his son, Joseph, ran it until his death in 2020. Joe's widow, Carolyn, owns and operates the landmark.

is West Virginia's oldest continuously operated general store by a whisker—O'Hurley's inception date is a close second. Harper's owners have preserved most of the store's original fixtures and materials, from the worn, oiled floorboards to the dingy tin ceiling; from the brass, circa-1910 cash register that still worked to the oak-framed candy case manufactured by M.L. Himn a century ago.

Joe told me that this dichotomy explains how two small retailers survive at a rural crossroads. There is no sense in trying to be everything to everyone. Harper's and Yokum's each own a niche, and each does a splendid job of filling it.

Yokum's appeal is to the traveler looking for quick service and convenience. Harper's caters to the experiential shopper, the person willing to give his eyes a few minutes to adjust to the dim light and dark fixtures, his mind a pause to comprehend the gigantic step back in time.

Harper's is for the person who wants to meet the owner and spend a few minutes or an hour talking about weather, gas prices, local history, or even politics. It's also for the biker or outdoor enthusiast who wants a T-shirt that melds souvenir with personal interests. It is part museum and

Joe and Carolyn Harper in their Seneca Rocks store, May 2008. Even the 1910 cash register was vintage general-store stock. D.C. Harper acquired it in 1925 when he bought out the Parsons Pulp & Paper store at Horton.

part store. Just inside the door was what appeared to be a large pickle jar with a couple of bear claws preserved in formaldehyde.

"My dad (Bardon "Buck") kind of put out the word that he'd like to have bear paws to show people, and one morning he came down to open the store and there they were on the porch," Joe said.

The bear motif was repeated farther inside the store, where a 5-foot-tall stuffed black bear towered over a souvenir counter. Joe Harper shot the bear on May 17, 1983. It was retribution for killing Harper's sheep, just as the stuffed coyote and bobcat in the store were victims of pest control.

Joe Harper's interest in killing vermin spoke to his other line of work as the largest sheep farmer in the state and one of the state's largest cattle farmers. Joe said the Alleghenies have the finest pastureland in the United States and produce equally fine livestock. But attacks from coyotes and bears take huge bites out of profits.

Just as Joe Harper was adamant about shielding his investment in livestock, he carried on the Harper tradition of protecting the family's retailing interests by forecasting and responding to economic and cultural

Joe Harper stands in the doorway of his general store while his daughter-in-law, Ashley Harper, and youngsters enjoy frozen treats. From left: granddaughter Cali Harper, her friend Carly Cooper, and grandson Cole Harper. May 2008.

trends. When his great grandfather, J. M., started Harper's, it was a true general store that stocked homestead and farm essentials—farming tools to sewing needles, livestock supplies to fabric.

"Roads weren't that good, and a lot of people didn't have a car," Joe said, explaining the local retailing environment that once supported three general stores. "This is a little hub here, there's only one avenue that goes west (through the mountains) and it's right here."

As with Joe, J. M. Harper also farmed in the valley and built structures still in use.

"He was smart. He did some engineering feats that are phenomenal," Joe said of his grandfather, who went to Marshall College. "I keep (the buildings that J. M. built) maintained. I couldn't replace them."

His great-grandfather had the store for about 10 years, when his son, D. C., came over from Piedmont and bought it. Foreseeing transportation's future, D. C. became a Standard Oil dealer in 1914. The store was Exxon's oldest retail outlet in West Virginia until the oil giant's unfavorable policies toward small outlets forced Joe to exit their game.

Joe Harper took a break to talk with me about the store and its history back in May 2008. We sat in a booth in his restaurant that looks out toward the rocks that once belonged to his father, Buck Harper, but were taken from the family through eminent domain in 1968.

When D. C. began to offer gasoline, the product was packaged in barrels that had to be hauled in with horse and wagon from Petersburg. A spigot inserted into the barrel was used to dispense the gasoline into a one-gallon container, from which the buyer transferred the fuel to his car's tank.

D. C. Harper initially sold only a few gallons of gas a month, but he saw the future of travel and became a Ford dealer. He also became a farm machinery dealer as mechanization replaced the horse. By 1920, he had to install a 275-gallon gasoline storage tank and hand pump to provide fuel for all the equipment he'd sold.

When electricity came to the valley, D. C. responded by stocking refrigerators, fans, freezers, light fixtures, and the wiring and hardware necessary to make them run.

D.C. owned the store until 1964, when he became ill and agreed to sell the stock to his son, Bardon "Buck" Harper, who had it until 1984. Joe said his father was a visionary in the vein of his father and grandfather. He foresaw the tourism boom and, with several other men, started the Potomac Highland Tourism Council. Buck served as president three times. His son continued in the tradition and served as president of the board.

It was under Buck Harper's watch that Seneca Rocks and nearly 400 acres of surrounding land passed from Harper family ownership to the U.S. Government. Most of the land around the rocks had been owned by Major Sampson Sites (1824-1910), who had served in the Confederate Army. Buck Harper's grandfather , Joseph Martin Harper, married Sites' daughter, Anna Apppenson, in 1885. She inherited the valuable property. D.C. Harper, their only son who survived to adulthood, purchased the dower rights of John Sites' widow in 1930 and acquired the rocks and all the land in front of it.

The federal government, allegedly concerned that Buck Harper and his heirs would develop the rocks for commercial use, condemned them in 1968 and, through eminent domain, offered $7,919 to the affected landowners. Buck took the government to court, but Joe said the settlement was not much more than the original offer after paying all the legal fees. It has remained a sore spot for generations.

The Harpers made the best of the rocks' public ownership and built upon this popularity with outdoor-recreation enthusiasts while continuing a tradition of caring for established clients. The store's earliest morning

The Harper's Store mascot pooch rests by the heater on a chilly morning in May 2008 while Joe Harper visits with one of the regulars who stop in for news and coffee.

customers were usually locals passing on their way to work or an appointment in Petersburg or Elkins. Buck Warner, a former sheriff of Pendleton County, stopped most mornings to get a cup of coffee and catch up on the news with Joe. Like many of the long-established customers here, Buck could tell Joe to chalk up his purchases to the credit account and he'd settle with him later.

"One time I paid him $589," Buck told me. "It was getting up there a little too high."

Buck, who grew up in the Seneca Rocks region, moved to D.C. to make his living. After 25 years in the city, he moved back in 1985 and discovered the store had changed little in his absence. "It's pretty much the same store," he said. "It's a store that's got just about everything you need and some things you don't need."

Joe said he continued his grandfather's approach to shop keeping: "We're too small to stock a lot, but what we have will be of good quality."

"If you don't see it, ask for it," Joe said. "We probably got it."

Before I departed the store for more wanderings, Joe Harper told me there was one additional reason that the two retailers had co-existed for a century. Back in the early days, general stores often hosted the Post Office, and getting the contract was a matter of political connections. "The Blands were Democrats, and the Harpers were Republican," Joe said. Depending upon which party was in power, either Bland's or Harper's store would host the post office and be guaranteed traffic for at least four years.

Politics aside, Joe said this coexistence for generations was a testimony to both the owners' ingenuity and the two families' ability to get along with each other.

"We're friends and we don't bicker back and forth," he said. "My wife and I go down and eat at Shirley's restaurant from time to time. This (community) is too little; you can't be fighting and bickering back and forth."

Joseph Oliver Harper died February 19, 2020. Carolyn, his widow, continues to own and operate the business.

Attached to cables and stepping on iron rungs, adventure seekers begin their ascent of Nelson's Rocks on the via ferrata.

Along the Way: Nelson Rocks

The scariest hike I ever made while wandering West Virginia was at Nelson Rocks, another Tuscarora sandstone formation in Pendleton County. Comparable to Seneca in height and challenges, Nelson Rocks are as obscure as the former are famous. The formation is hidden from traffic on Route 28. Travel down Nelson Gap Road about a mile, then turn around and head back toward the highway to catch the breathtaking sight of the twin razor-back fins of sandstone jutting above the hardwoods.

Like its famous sister formation to the north, Nelson Rocks were in private ownership for decades. If climbing was done on them, it was low key and through a network of adventure seekers who obtained permission from the landowner. But in 1997, Nelson Rocks came on the market to settle an estate, and Maryland rock climbing enthusiasts Stu and LaVonne Hammett purchased the craggy landmark. The following year, the family opened two miles of trails. It was a bittersweet year—Stu's father died of cancer approximately six months prior to the purchase; two weeks after closing, Stu found his 8-year-old son, Pierson, dead in his bed.

"I went in to wake him up for school and he had died in his sleep," Stu told me in an interview back in 2007.

The day prior to closing the deal, Pierson had bushwhacked a trail up on the west side of the fins. Pierson's contribution is thus memorialized by the trail that bears his name; a cut-off that goes to an overlook bears the name of their daughter, Gracie.

The couple's need to make Nelson Rocks a profitable venture and accessible to more climbers led to establishing West Virginia's first via ferrata. Popular in Europe, a via ferrata uses a system of iron rungs permanently embedded in the rocks and a safety harness attached to a steel cable that runs along the face of the rock near the rungs. As the climber progresses along the predetermined route, he or she is always attached to the cable. If a climber slips or falls, the maximum distance dropped is only a few feet.

And, yes, people actually do this at heights of hundreds of feet.

"(Humans) are designed for physical and mental challenge in an outdoor environment," Stu told me, explaining the lure of climbing. "Climbing is an approximation of that, and that's rare in this day and age."

Nelson's Rocks offers outstanding, rugged scenery for those who also enjoy strenuous, heart-pounding adventure.

A French company installed the United States' first via ferrata in Kentucky, but Stu couldn't afford them. Avid climbers themselves, the couple turned to their circle of adventurous friends for assistance. In a span of six months in 2002, they strung a half-mile of 3/8-inch steel cable and installed 250 bolts and 185 steel rungs on sections of the two fins. They also built a 250-foot long swinging bridge suspended more than 150 feet above the rock-strewn corridor trail. Climbers are hooked to the safety cable as they traverse the swaying bridge.

The Hammetts opened the via ferrata in June 2002 and ran it until 2009, when they sold the operation to John Hall, owner of Endless Horizons, a Harrisonburg, Virginia company. Hall re-branded the site as NROCKS and expanded the operation with a new welcome center, lodging options, and zip canopy tour.

The day I was there in 2007, Stu explained that he was no longer able to climb the rocks like he once did (he'd broken his back on a climb elsewhere years earlier), and they were looking for a buyer.

Stu offered to let me climb the via ferrata, but I chose instead to "enjoy" the views from one of the hiking trails that ascend the rock fins. Prior to my departure on this self-directed hike, Stu advised me to keep my eyes open for rattlesnakes and copperheads—as if my fear of heights was insufficient to put me on high alert.

That "hike" reminded me that I was now over 50 years of age. It left me breathless and there were times I was shaking from the exertion and the fear of encountering a poisonous—O.K., any—snake. The scariest segment of the trek was downhill through a field of large rocks and boulders, perfect habitat for reptiles. Fortunately, a climber who was returning to home base via that route offered to lead the way.

I never returned to the via ferrata; as much as I love sweeping views of the Allegheny Mountains, seeing them from a fin of Tuscarora sandstone while literally shaking in my hiking boots was adventure overload. Call me a coward, but I have since limited my wanderings to more sedate subjects, such as covered bridges and gristmills.

For whatever reasons, the *GOLDENSEAL* editor at that time didn't purchase the story, making all that exertion, worry, and fear financially unrewarding, as well.

Online: NROCKS Outdoor Adventures, nrocks.com.

Silas Kirk greets guests at his 100th birthday party, April 27, 2012, near his home in Rivesville, Marion County. One of 15 children, Silas had a very difficult childhood, followed by many years of struggling as an adult. Faith and hard work got him through it.

Chapter 5

Silas Kirk's Century

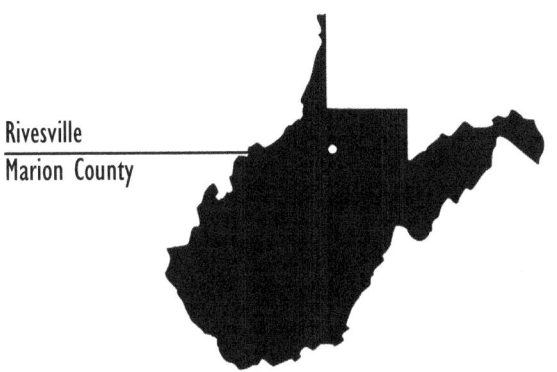

Rivesville
Marion County

The value of a penny has fallen so low, most of us figure it's not worth the risk to stop, stoop, and snatch one from the ground. But Silas Hoover Kirk could not look at a penny without thinking of its value to him as a youngster.

"My brother was 12 years older than me, and he was corresponding with some of the girls, and we lived about a mile and a half from the mailbox," the Rivesville resident once told me. "And he would say, 'Silas, I will give you a penny if you will get the mail.' That was three miles for one penny."

He estimated total earnings of about 50 cents on that private mail route, a job that taught him the value of money and simultaneously encouraged him to move into more profitable ventures that included farming, coal mining, brickyard labor, and excavation. And despite having worked "for himself" some of that time, Silas Kirk tells younger members of his family that "you never get to be your own boss. Even the president of the United States has people who tell him what to do."

I met the sage at his 100th birthday shindig, April 27, 2012. It was held at the Cross Roads Community Center, where he parceled out slices of

Silas Kirk listens to his daughter, Betty Jean Fast, speak about growing up under his care and guidance. The occasion was his 100th birthday celebration in 2012.

wisdom and anecdotes as thick and decadent as the slices of birthday cake his family served the guests. "Do what you know to do," he told the guests, taking a line from Dale Carnegie, one of his mentors.

Jesus Christ was another one.

"Jesus said, 'As ye would have men do to you, so you do unto them,'" Silas said, switching to evangelist mode. "Treat people right... the whole Bible is based on that one verse."

Ironically, the man who taught Silas much of what he knew about the Bible, his father Daniel Webster Kirk (1857-1930), set a poor example in the home.

"He knew his Bible, but he hated my guts from the day I was born. He never did like me, from the time I was a baby," said Silas, one of 15 children fathered by D.W. Kirk. Silas's mother, Clara Alice Annon Kirk (1874-1953), had 10 children by Daniel, who had fathered four others with a first wife, Mary Margaret Finch. She died from tuberculosis, and his second wife, Mollie A. Swiger Kirk, died delivering a stillborn child. All four of the children born to his first wife died of childhood diseases. D.W. Kirk buried two spouses and the five children in a span of four years; three of the children died within a four-month period.

Perhaps the pain of losing two wives and five offspring in such a short span turned Daniel Webster Kirk into a bitter, loveless man. "He was a good preacher, but if there was one place where he failed, it was on love. I don't remember a bit of love in his life," Silas said.

"(My father) could never work hard enough, long enough, to please his father," confirmed Bonnie Fast, one of Silas' six daughters. She said her paternal grandmother had a dream that illuminated that reality.

"In that dream, Grandma (Kirk) was stringing beans, and when she got done, she picked up what she thought was the pan of strings and tossed them out, but it was actually the infant Silas she tossed out onto the floor," Bonnie said. "Dad says he believes his father was thinking, 'I hope he's dead.' The pain of his father's rejection still haunts my dad to this day, and I believe my dad is trying to gain his father's love and approval at 100 years of age."

Silas told me that his father was always looking for a way to intimidate him. After Silas mastered reading the first primer, he proudly reported his accomplishment to his father. But Daniel Webster Kirk turned to the book's annotations intended for educators and told Silas he better be able read that text—or else.

"Think about a daddy putting pressure like that on a child ... if he had said, 'Little man, I'm proud of you, don't you,' see what a difference that would have made?" Silas said. "He never looked for the good."

The learning opportunities for a child growing up in rural West Virginia back then were further shortened by the agrarian economy. Silas was required to work on the family farm from sunrise to sunset. He often was absent from school, the term of which was limited to seven months to further accommodate the realities of subsistence farming.

"I was 14 years old and in the fifth grade. I never went back," Silas said.

'Bullheaded as a moose'

He compensated for the lack of education with determination, faith, and honesty, qualities that have defined many of Appalachia's great men and women who originated from humble beginnings.

"I was as bullheaded as a moose," Silas said. "I was honest, and when I went to work, the people were satisfied. My reputation is what got me through, and Jesus Christ stood by me the whole time. He stood by me and helped me."

Although Silas Kirk suffered from macular degeneration and could not be licensed to drive, he operated his lawn tractor around his property in Rivesville.

Silas was born at Levels Community but moved to the farm at Quiet Dell in Marion County when he was 2 years old. Silas said he rarely had any form of recreation as a child, and food was as scarce as charity in the Kirk home. He claimed that his longevity was a product of that difficult childhood.

"We were very limited in our (food options and variety). Dad had plenty to eat on the table, but he didn't have any care for choice," Silas said. "I don't think I had enough of the right kind of food to mature. I think I must have been 30 years old before I matured to manhood. I weighed 130 pounds and wore 30-30 pants for about 15 years."

Wild game was particularly scarce because people lived off the land.

"We ate every bit of the wild meat you could find," Silas said. "Ground hog, opossum, rabbit, squirrel. There were no deer at that time in West Virginia, I reckon. "

Recreation was in short supply, as well. "I was a hard worker and had to stay home and work on the farm. I got absolutely no recreation and no luxury, if any," Silas said.

Good footwear was among the luxuries Silas never knew as a child and young adult. He related a story of walking several miles to Fairmont for a

Silas Kirk's daughters sang a hymn for him as part of the 100th birthday celebration. From left are Clara Frances Spaid, Margaret May Hovatter, Mary Jane Forquer, Bonnie Louise Fast, Kathleen Anne Fike, and Betty Jean Fast.

Halloween celebration. His shoes were too small for his feet and inflicted great misery. Silas finally paused and cut a hole in the end of each shoe to provide relief to his tortured toes.

Silas went off the farm as young teenager and worked for other farmers at the rate of $1 a day.

"Hand mowing, haying, cutting wood, building fences and plowing," Silas said, listing the jobs he did. "Anything I could do. I worked from 7 a.m. until it was dark. They wanted your shirt wet with sweat when you quit. And if it rained that day, you only got 50 cents."

Silas met his future wife, Bertha Reynolds, at the Brethren Church where his father preached. Silas later served as pastor there, as well.

"(Bertha) was as pretty as a doll. I winked at her. I was about 8 years old. Everything grew from there," he said.

In 1930, Silas and Bertha eloped to Oakland, Maryland, shortly after Silas turned 18. She was 19. Silas did whatever he could to provide food

Silas Kirk leans in to listen to Bessie Vangilder, 96, while Hallie Williams, 90, and Blanche Collins (right), 94, await their opportunity to congratulate him.

for the family, but it was a hardscrabble life. Among the low points was when he discovered a ground hog in the woods that was half eaten by a fox. He brought home what remained of the carcass for his wife to cook.

"We even tried skunk, but it was too strong," he said. "It tasted just like it smells."

Virtually all working people in Marion County had money woes. Silas didn't have the money to pay the doctor so the doctor couldn't pay his dairy bill, and the dairyman could not pay his taxes. The doctor sent the dairyman to Silas' farm to take the family's only dairy cow.

"Before going to bed at night, my wife took off her only dress and washed it so it would be clean for the next day. She wore out straight-back chairs rocking the kids," Silas said. "Times were hard. Boy, I hope we don't ever have to go back to those times. I'll be leavin' soon, but I fear for you."

Silas signed up for a "relief job" with the Works Progress Administration to feed his family. "There were no government handouts, we had to work," he said.

The job was at the edge of Fairmont near the East Grafton Road and Homewood. "I had to walk several miles to work. They put me to work

Two days after his big party to mark a century of life, Silas Kirk pauses in the sunshine outside his home in Rivesville.

there and my father-in-law came to me and asked if it would be better for me if I transferred my job to his area at Glady Creek, near the Hebron Baptist Church. I said it sure it would, that was only a couple of miles from home. I was told that I had to bring some kind of tool to work with me and the only tool I had was a small mattock. I worked there for a couple of days digging soft sandstone, and it just ground the edge off our tools. So, they told us they were taking all of our tools to be sharpened. My father-in-law was a Democrat, and I was a Republican. He came to me and said he was going to lay me off. I said, 'What about my mattock?' He said, 'You don't have any mattock.'

"About 30 years later, when we were visiting the in-laws, (my father-in-law) disappeared and came back with an old dirt pick, which has a hoe on one end about an inch wide and a pick on the other end. He asked if I had any use for it. After thinking about it, I realized he was trying to pay me back for stealing my mattock. That is about as dirty as a man could get. My own father-in-law."

From coal to bricks

The difficulties inherent to making a living during the Great Depression were compounded by a lack of transportation, adequate clothing, and basic household needs.

"I did not even have a clock. And we were supposed to go about two miles to work, and half a mile of that was through the woods," Silas said. "So I woke up one time during the night, and I said, 'Bertha will you get up and get me something to eat and to put in my bucket for dinner?' We both got up, and I ate some breakfast. I walked out in the yard and looked around, and it was black as black cats. I had no clock, had no idea what time it was. I went back in the house and sat down on the bed and rolled over backwards and went to sleep. After a while I woke up. I said, 'I got to go, I got to get there'. I started out through the woods . . . feeling for the path with my feet. I finally got to work, and it was getting daylight when I got there."

The walking was made all the more difficult by a lack of proper shoes.

"My shoes were wore clear out, until my toes were sticking through my shoes. And I got enough money, just by pinching around this place and that place, to get me a new pair of shoes," Silas said. "I went into Walter and Highland beside the H & H Drug Store on Adams Street in Fairmont, and I told the man what I wanted . . . I said, 'I'm going to take these (old shoes) off,' and I put them new shoes on and handed the old ones to the man and said, 'You can throw these in the garbage.' He looked at me like I was crazy. He said, 'You can leave them shoes here. Somebody can wear those shoes. There are men coming in here every day with shoes worse than that.'"

Silas eventually found work in the coal mines at Barrackville.

"Seven dollars a day! Oh boy, I was getting rich now," Silas said. "I was doing real good. But there was still no money to get ahold of to buy anything. Every bank in Fairmont had gone under."

One of his children's teachers told Silas that an elderly farmer had a small stash of cash and was cashing her paychecks. He did the same for Silas, until the mine owners brought cash in from Pittsburgh. Silas recalls a blacksmith keeping guard over the payroll transaction with a sawed-off shotgun.

Silas Kirk's farm property included this lovely waterfall, which members hiked to as part of their celebration of his 100th birthday in 2012. The land owners gave permission to the family to hike to the secluded spot.

With a reliable income from mining, Silas kept the commitment he made to his mother back in 1930, when his father died. Silas had promised to buy the family farm at Quiet Dell, and with a steady paycheck coming in he bought about 80 acres for $1,000. He had to pay $100 annually for the land. But times were so tough in that first year, Silas was unable to keep his commitment. Indeed, Silas didn't even have the money to pay the gas bill.

"While we were in the Depression, we had natural gas to cook with and we used wood to heat with. My gas bill was 50 cents a month, and I could not pay it. So, I sent a letter to them, it was the most pitiful letter you ever seen, and they didn't shut off the gas," he said.

In addition to the Barrackville mine, Silas worked at the Kilarm, Carolina, and Consol No. 93 Jordan mines. He hired on as a driver of horses, which were still being used to haul coal out of the mines. But he really wanted to load slate or coal. He got his break at the Carolina mine, where Silas set a record for the company, shoveling 35 tons of coal in a 7 ½-hour shift.

Working at that pace and in a time of high demand, Silas earned up to $300 in 15 days. But after the war, mechanization resulted in the wholesale loss of mining jobs. Silas decided to try working at the Hammond Brickyard, which was closer to his home at Quiet Dell than the mines were.

His job was moving bricks by wheelbarrow—the pay was 7 cents per load of 100 bricks, which were manually loaded/unloaded. While working there, he purchased the bricks to build his family's seven-bedroom house on the farm. Each family member pitched in on the project, recalled Bonnie Fast.

"His idea was to build a house that was maintenance free," Bonnie said. To that end, the exterior was brick and the roof metal. "We lived in the basement but slept on the second floor," she said.

Silas returned to the coal mines when it became evident that the brickyard was in its final days. He was working the midnight shift when the big snow of Thanksgiving 1950 hit the region. Silas found a ride from Consol No. 93 Jordan Mine to Walnut Grove, from which point he trudged the remaining five miles to his home. After eating dinner, Silas decided to check on the welfare of two elderly folks, siblings John and Mary Rudy, who lived across the field.

Silas rode his horse to their home, where he found them huddled around a fading ember to keep warm. Silas assessed the situation and began hauling in water and coal. He said John and Mary had resigned themselves to just "sit there and freeze." Silas returned the next day and hauled in a large supply of coal, which he piled in the corner of one room.

When his mining work once again became unreliable, Silas turned to being his own boss. He purchased a front-end loader and started installing septic systems and doing other excavation and construction jobs.

"I really put my life into it," he said. "I did pretty good at it and made a lot of friends."

The blessing of children

Silas and Bertha had nine children: Darrell Willie, Howard Ezra (died in infancy), Margaret May (Hovatter), Clara Frances (Spaid), Kathleen Ann (Fike), Bonnie Louise (Fast), Mary Jane (Forquer), Betty Jean (Fast), and John Mark Kirk.

Decades after Howard Ezra died, Silas still recalled those mournful days. He said the baby contracted summer complaint from consuming sour milk.

"One of my babies was born on the 21st, died on the 29th and was buried

Silas Kirk's surviving children surround him for a photo at his 100th birthday celebration in 2012. From left are Margaret May Hovatter, Clara Frances Spaid, Kathleen Anne Fike, Bonnie Louise Fast, Mary Jane Forquer, Betty Jean Fast, and John Mark Kirk.

the 30th of May," Silas said. "It just poured down the rain the night he died, and hail fell, an awful bunch of hail. There was a pile of hail alongside the building the next day."

His wife also had a miscarriage, and Silas recalled placing the fetus in a quart jar and burying it on the farm.

Silas said the best memories of his life are of times spent with his children. He recalls working until midnight in the coal mine, purchasing a half gallon of ice cream, and waking his family to enjoy the treat.

"I'd come home at 1 or 2 in the morning, and I'd holler, 'Ice cream!' The kids would come running like a bunch of hungry rats. That's what you call precious memories," Silas said.

One Christmas, Silas saved enough money to purchase a case of Coca-Cola, 24 small bottles. Unfortunately, the family also consumed about four pounds of fresh wintergreen berries. The youngsters munched on the fresh berries Christmas Eve, and when Christmas Day arrived, they were all too ill to enjoy their Christmas Cokes.

As for the most difficult years of his life, Silas said they were the last four or five years of his first wife's life, when she suffered from dementia. "She got so where she was mad at me day and night for several years," he said. "It was pretty rough, I tell you."

Bertha later had colon cancer and lymphoma. She died in April 1989. Silas remarried after just six months of being a widower. He and his second wife, Lillian, had 15 years together.

Silas' children said that their father always expected them to work hard on the farm when they were growing up. He instilled Christian values in them and was proud to say not one of them had divorced.

He lived his faith, consistently putting God and others ahead of himself. When he was just 22 years old, Silas was called upon by his older brother, George, to assist a poor family whose infant was mortally ill. Silas walked about a mile to get to the family's home, which was back in the woods.

"I said, 'You care if I pick the baby up?' 'No, won't hurt a thing. Doctor says he'll be dead in the morning, anyways.' So, I picked the baby up and he was wet all around his waist and cold. I said, 'Get some dry clothes, let's dry this kid up.' They got some dry clothes and we put some on the baby. I said, 'You got any ginger? Any lard?'

"I made ginger and lard plaster, like my mother used to use. I put a patch on his chest and a patch on his back. 'I said you got any onions?' 'Yeah.' 'O.K. get me some onions. Slice the onions, put them in a skillet with a little bit of sugar and water. Bring them almost up to a boil, and we give that to the baby for pneumonia.'

"We gave that baby some of that stuff that night. They got his bottle, and I said, 'Let's get more milk in this kid.' And we did that, and the baby, after he got dry clothes on, something to eat, he went to sleep. I think he lived to be 65, and he was going to be dead in the morning."

The man was Everett Vangilder, whose sister, Marge, attended Silas' 100th birthday celebration and corroborated the story—she was 10 or 12 at the time and was the one who sliced the onions.

During Silas' 100th birthday party, many of his children, grandchildren, and in-laws reminisced about their favorite memories of growing up under his guidance. Bob Orosz of Temple, Florida, married Silas' granddaughter, Sandra. He described Silas as "a character" who took his responsibilities seriously and kept his word.

"My favorite story of his is when was given the responsibility of being the executor of a will. He had to stay up all night with a guy named Hans, protecting the will, because some of the heirs wanted to destroy it, because without the will, there would be no legal way to distribute the estate. He said, 'If you give somebody your word, you better consider all the implications, because it might take more than you think to fulfill it.'"

Bob can't remember ever hearing Silas complain about himself or all the hardships he had in his life. But he was one to share his wisdom. His granddaughter, Veronica Fast Higgs, said Silas taught her a saying that's she tried to follow all her life: "Once a task has once begun, never leave it before it's done. If the task be great or small, do it right, or not at all."

She observed that her grandfather's diet flew in the face of modern preventive health teaching.

"He loves fat. He had to have some kind of animal fat with every meal, to soften up his bread," she said.

At the age of 100, Silas still lived in his Rivesville home. Hard of hearing, he put a sign on his door telling visitors to "make a lot of noise" to get him to the door. Macular degeneration prevented him from driving a car, but he still drove his riding lawnmower around the yard for recreation. Bonnie Fast said that if it had not for his poor eyesight, Silas would still be using his computer to stay in touch with family, read the Bible, and research family history. He loved to learn and taught himself to use a computer at the age of 90.

Silas said he was richer than the legendary King Solomon. "Solomon did not have a car that can go over 100 miles per hour with air conditioning and heat," Silas said. "He did not have a refrigerator, a gas furnace, or a computer."

He entered his second century of life prepared for the inevitable. He requested that his burial be in a box made of plywood as a tribute to America's fallen soldiers—he did not want a casket that was better than anything a soldier would be buried in A family member had already built the casket and delivered it the funeral home.

Silas Kirk died August 22, 2013, at the age of 101. In keeping with his wishes, his daughter, Bonnie, conducted the funeral service. She had performed the ceremony when Silas married Lillian, and Silas told her, "You married me, I want you to bury me!" Bonnie said.

Century No. 2 along Route 119 in northern Barbour County is marked with a road sign, but finding Century No. 1 can be a challenge. Not much is left of the former coal-mining towns, and those who reside there are largely unaware of their tragic story.

Chapter 6

Two Centuries

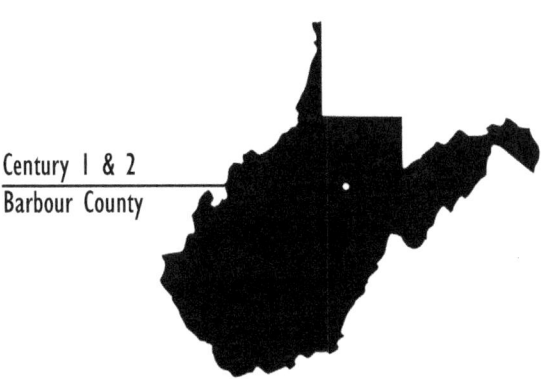

Century 1 & 2
Barbour County

The highway sign told me that I had reached "Century No. 2" on a stretch of Route 119 in northern Barbour County, raising a series of questions in my mind: "Where is Century No. 1?" "Why not just give it another name and avoid the confusion?" "Why name a town 'Century' in the first place?"

Driving through Century No. 2, it was evident the town was not the result of urban sprawl. Aside from the ubiquitous signs of coal mining, including what were clearly once company houses, there was little industry and commerce there. A deceased shop, "J&S Grocery and Flea Market," stood at the intersection of Big Run Road and Route 119. A stone's throw away was Century's watering hole, Den Lin's Bar and Restaurant, marked by the town's singular LED sign. Next to it was the Good 2 Go Convenience Store, which had a lunch counter where friends Pete Winters, Amanda Delauter, and Albert "Almost a Rose" Thorn refreshed themselves.

They were quick to accommodate my presence and answer my questions about a town that neither called home but nevertheless found it a good place to gather.

Good 2 Go patrons can fish in the pond outside the convenience store in Century No. 2

"Everybody gets together here," Amanda said while she waited for her sandwich to come off the grill. Pete urged me to order a Philly steak sandwich; I danced around the suggestion, not wanting to disclose to this carnivorous group that I'm a vegan. I returned the conversation to the town's odd name, which sparked a discussion among the trio.

"I just heard that story the other day," Pete said. "It goes back to when they discovered coal up in Century No. 1. They said they had discovered enough coal to last a century. And when they found out there was more coal here, they said there was enough for century number two."

Railroad tracks parallel the highway, and I asked the diners if they ever see any trains recently run on them. Amanda said the nearest rail traffic is at the sand plant. "You can hear them from here," she said. But years, perhaps decades, have passed since a train hauled a load of Century coal on these tracks.

"They tried to open the deep mines four miles up the road," Amanda said. "There are plenty of seams left back up in here."

They shared stories of family members who worked in the mines and suffered injury, of picking coal for the family's stove out of the gob pile as a child, and of the general hard times the area had fallen upon. Amid all

Century No. 1 retains its heritage of being a mining town with the United Mine Workers of American union hall in what was once the elementary school.

those stories, the mystery of Century's name hung unanswered over our conversation like the collective smoke from their cigarettes.

I asked directions to the town of Century No. 1. It turns out I'd passed it on the way in; a sign pointing to a community center, where a jam session is held every Sunday afternoon, was where I needed to turn.

A mile or so down this back road I came upon Century No. 1, one more lonely leftover of the mining industry. The most prominent building in the community was the white UMWA hall; the structure was built as an elementary school but became surplus when the new school opened in Volga, north of Century No. 2.

A woman who lived in a former company house on the hill overlooking the hall told me that the miners' organization still owned the building and rented it out for parties. She'd lived there 36 years with her husband, and had no idea how the towns got their names. She knew coal was their legacy and, if the mines were to re-open, coal would be their salvation, although not for them. Her husband worked on the strip mine, but he was now on disability.

She said there used to be a tipple for loading coal at Century No. 1, but it and the tracks had been gone for decades.

I stopped at a couple of other houses in both Century No. 1 and Century No. 2, but no one was home. I continued north, toward my motel room, where I turned to the Internet to shed light on this mystery.

Through an article on the West Virginia Department of Arts, Culture and History website, I learned that the Century Coal Company of Pittsburgh. Century began producing coal from a shaft mine at Century No. 1 in 1901. Century No. 2 was a slope mine that came later.

At 4:30 p.m., March 22, 1906, an explosion in No. 1's shaft mine resulted in 23 deaths. According to a state report issued later that year, 11 of the men were killed by direct force of the explosion, the other 12 perished in the mine's poisonous gases. The 12 men were rescued but died from "fright or acute insanity," most likely from the carbon monoxide, the report noted. "This subject had the delusion that the roof was about to fall upon him and constantly pleaded to be removed from this imaginary danger," the report stated.

Another man retrieved from the mine died from the shock of having his crushed legs amputated. The motorman, unaware of the explosion, ran the trip of 16 loaded cars into the affected section, plowing into and running over miners trying to escape the inferno.

I thought of the wailing that must have echoed through Century No. 1 that night. I thought of the wives and children who soon would be forced to move out of the company housing because more miners and their families would be moving in to replace the deceased husbands and fathers.

The echoes are long gone; folks who lived around there didn't know about the deceased miners, their widows, or Century's dark fame. To them, Century No. 1 and No. 2 were but tombstones resting on a rich seam of coal in which 23 lives were snuffed more than a century ago.

Chapter 7

Mail Call in Glady

Bemis & Glady
Randolph County

The weekday highlight for most residents of Glady came at 2 p.m. That's when Calvin Hansbrough Shifflett hollered "MAIL'S UP" from behind a wall of brass mailboxes that had served the hamlet since September 14, 1886, when this Randolph County community received postal recognition.

Officially, Calvin was assistant postmaster of Glady; his wife, Frances was postmaster. But it was generally Calvin whom the postal patrons of 26268 saw and dealt with when they stopped at the post office/general store. Ten miles south of Route 33, the dual-function building stood a few hundred yards beyond the crossroads of Bemis and Glady roads.

Serving as assistant postmaster was just one of Calvin's interests. He also was proprietor of the general store that shared space with the post office, and he and his wife ran a little store in Bemis that mirrored the Glady store's product line, except the Bemis store sold beer.

"I can't sell beer here in the post office," Calvin told me when I wandered into his domain in September 2006. "I get people who ask for it, and I got a ready answer: 'Did you ever see any post office that sold beer?'"

Calvin was all for selling and consuming beer in the right place and

Calvin Shifflett, assistant postmaster at the Glady Post Office, catches up on the news while awaiting the mail to arrive from the Clarksburg distribution center. September 2006.

time. On Fridays, Saturdays, and Sundays, he worked as bartender of his 50-seat bar known to patrons as "Calvin's." He also was known to pick up his guitar and entertain those guests on Saturday nights.

"I'm on the job seven days a week, I don't have no days off," said Calvin, who was 72 when I spent the day with him in Glady.

A former lumber town that had three sawmills in its heyday, Glady is a crossroads hamlet whose residents include a mix of elderly life-long residents, younger people who drive to Elkins to work, and seasonal visitors with summer cottages and general delivery post office boxes. A Columbia Gas compressor station a short distance from the hamlet provided a steady stream of workers, vehicular traffic, and business for Calvin's store. The hamlet and Calvin's enterprises also benefited from the town being a crossroads for hiking trails.

Calvin also sold gasoline until 2003, but mandated upgrades to his pumps would have cost him $7,000, and he decided it was more profitable not to sell gas than invest in more infrastructure.

The Glady store and post office maintained the same hours: 10 a.m. to 4 p.m., Monday through Saturday, closed on Sundays. Six hours a day sufficed for taking care of whatever business had to be done in Glady.

The Glady Post Office and Calvin's store were housed in an 18-by-18-foot frame building. The division of function was well defined; as one entered the front and only door, Calvin's store was to the left and consisted of a small freezer for ice, beverage cooler, a candy case topped by a sales counter, and a wall covered with shelves for canned goods, convenience foods, medicinal needs, and canning supplies (home gardening and canning were major pastimes in Glady).

Postal business was conducted on the right-hand side of the building. The post office consisted of a long counter whereupon rested a fax machine, desktop computer, and row of dual-combination postal boxes with two tiny clerk windows, one of them with bars. The one-piece unit still bore the original "Sadler Company" gold-letter logo.

A brown kerosene stove stood at the room's rear and was flanked by wooden chairs. The oak one directly right of the heater came from the old Bemis schoolhouse. A stack of newspapers on a bar stool next to the chair provided Calvin with updates from Elkins and Harrisonburg, which Calvin consumed as he tipped his chair against the wall. An adjacent brown recliner had been Calvin's seat of choice until a bum hip and arthritis made it difficult for him to exit the thing. He abdicated his sitting rights to patrons who wanted to wait for their mail or shoot the breeze in upholstered comfort.

The dichotomy of this building, which Calvin leased to the United

Calvin Shifflett stands outside his general store/post office in the Randolph County crossroads of Glady, September 2006.

States Postal System, is something postal inspectors frowned upon, as were the chairs, which might encourage loitering. Calvin said loitering in the post office was as much a tradition as periodic postal-rate increases.

"Yeah, they don't like it too well," he said. "When we took over here, the guy called me over and told me, 'You shouldn't allow them to sit around here.' So I got my sign up."

Thus, on the front of his building Calvin posted a hand-lettered "no loitering" sign next to the Pepsi thermometer and "Report Deer and Bear Kills Here" notice. Loitering wasn't the only issue that his D.C. bosses had with how Calvin executed his agreement.

"They complained on a couple of visits about having a store in here," he said. "They let me know one time that they weren't happy about it. And I said, 'I'll just lease half of (the building) to you,' and they said, 'No you won't!'" Calvin simply "borrowed" the store's half, just as he borrowed the telephone land line that was for official business only. However, with Calvin's place being the center of Glady commerce, all manner of inquiries came through this line. "Is the mail up?" "What's the weather like there?" "Any deer being checked in?"

When the phone was installed, postal authorities directed him to answer it, "Glady Post Office."

When he was not sorting mail, checking in deer, or answering the phone, Calvin Shifflett took care of the general store that shared the building with the post office. He was the landlord and the assistant postmaster.

"I told them whenever you start telling me how to answer the phone, you can start paying the bill," Calvin said.

A telephone and Internet connection—Glady went online in 2004—were essential to running a post office, no matter how small, because of the many reports that must be generated and filed daily. Information about scanned items, such as certified and mail sent with delivery confirmation, also required electronic tracking.

"I do every report that Elkins does," Calvin said. "You would think that they would have different rules for us small offices, but they don't."

The post office had the capacity for 30 box patrons, but only 22 boxes were rented the week I was there. There were several general delivery accounts and 23 Bemis postal patrons who received their mail through Glady. A contract mail carrier delivered mail three times a week on a two-mile run out of Glady. Gene Cave drove the route that had just 10 patrons, two of them commercial accounts that justified the excursion.

"The route used to go 15 miles to the Sinks of Gandy," Calvin said. "That's the way it was 100 years ago when they delivered it by mule. Old-man Andrew Tingler carried mail on a mule and horseback."

Calvn Shifflett calls a Glady postal patron to the window for his mail.

Getting established

Calvin became a post office landlord in 1961. His mother-in-law, Susie Hedrick, was postmaster at Bemis when that office and Glady merged. She had the opportunity to go to Glady, but a new building was needed. Calvin built it from recycled lumber.

"She had a whole basement full of used lumber, so this was built with used lumber," he said. "A fellow up the road, Delbert Strawder, built it for them. He was a retired railroader."

The structure was simple, with a rough floor of unfinished boards preserved by years of dirt ground into their fiber. It lacked indoor plumbing, but Calvin also owned an adjacent house with the amenity. But visitors who asked to use a restroom were directed to an outhouse behind the house.

When his mother-in-law died in 1976, Calvin and his wife decided to take on the postal duties out of their concern that the system would pull the plug on this rural outpost if they had to find new personnel. The job wasn't particularly strenuous, the hours decent, and stress minimal except in hunting season. That's when the store and deer-check station hopped with business to the point Calvin struggled to get the mail up on time.

Glady postal patrons gather around the heating stove on a September day in 2007 as they wait for Calvin Shifflett to put up the mail. The post office was on the right side of the building, his general store on the left.

Most of the mail that came through Glady was the prosaic stuff that ends up in a landfill, but occasionally something addressed to Israel arrived because Glady's ZIP code and that of an Israeli town were identical. Even parcels addressed to Israel got misrouted to Glady.

"The carrier brought it this one package and she was complaining how bad it smelled," he said. It contained very ripe fish.

"I took it out and put it in an outbuilding until the next morning, then I sent it back with a big mark around (the code). That fish took the long route. It should have gone to Israel and it went to Glady," he said.

The Glady Post Office delivered 100 pieces of mail on an average day, but rarely took in more than a dozen pieces of outgoing. Glady mail came through Clarksburg by way of Bowden. Wilmoth Lambert, a contract carrier, brought the mail to Glady. Calvin could set his watch by Wilmoth, whose white vehicle generally crested the hill at 1:40 p.m. each weekday.

About 10 minutes before the big event, Roy Rhodes parked across the street from the post office and waited for Wilmoth's arrival. Roy followed Wilmoth into the post office, where he took up his post against the general store counter while Wilmoth and Calvin sorted the mail. Earl Bonnell, another postal patron, took a seat next to the brown kerosene stove and beneath the back window. Gene Cave was next to arrive. The men chatted about the weather, happenings around the area, and the status of their gardens while they waited for Calvin to announce "MAIL'S UP!"

Earl made a beeline for box 112, Roy for box 83. Gene headed out the door with the mail for his 10-patron route. Earl and Roy flipped through their stacks of mail, bade farewell to Calvin, and headed home.

Throughout the afternoon, another eight to 10 patrons wandered in to check their boxes and perhaps drop off a letter or parcel. Calvin closed the post office at 4 p.m. and headed to his home across the mountain in Bemis.

Bemis was where Calvin got his first sense of just how significant the arrival of mail is to an individual—that daily dose of anticipation that perhaps one's ship has finally come in via that mythical check that's been in the mail for years or that Publishers Clearing House Sweepstakes notice. Or perhaps it was a entitlement check or letter from a grandchild. Whatever he delivered, the mailman was the common man's most dependable ray of hope against mediocrity's banal skies.

"That's the only excitement there is here, mail time," Calvin said. "That's the way it was when I was a kid. The train would come into Bemis at 12:15 (p.m.). There would be 30 to 40 people down there waiting for the train to come in."

Boys gathered at the station to lug the mail bags from the train to the post office. Sacks stuffed with Sears Roebuck catalogs were especially heavy. Calvin opted for carrying the bags containing letters.

Calvin's memory of the Western Maryland train's arrival at Bemis is one of wartime, when 50 of the community's young men were serving their country. It seemed as if the train was always either taking a young man to war or delivering a disabled veteran or his remains.

Calvin's family, from Virginia, settled in Glady in 1925. "My Dad came over in 1916 and worked for the Western Maryland Railroad, all his brothers were section foremen on the railroad," Calvin said. His father went back to Virginia in 1918, but later returned to West Virginia.

By then Joseph and Rosa Shifflett had three boys—Medford, Ronald, and Maynard. Three more—Orville, Clarence, and Calvin—were born in West Virginia.

Mail arrived in Bemis by train and the natural resources of the heavily forested region left by the same. Logging was the main industry. *West Virginia and Regional History Center at WVU.*

If there existed a common thread in this family, it was the members' ability to play just about any stringed instrument. "All of us played except my one brother," he said. "My father played, and my uncle who played with us played the banjo, fiddle, and guitar. It just came natural to us."

Anything that entered or left Bemis did so on a train back then. The school, which offered grades one through 10, was the center of recreation and social life. His mother, who had only an eighth-grade education, taught Calvin his ABCs and how to read. She convinced the principal that Calvin was sufficiently prepared to enter school a year early, and the time he was 14, Calvin was in high school.

"Things were pretty tough," Calvin said. "My dad had an accident and broke his leg, and things were pretty tough when I was going to high school." Hungry and inspired by his older brothers who served in the Navy during World War II, Calvin conspired to enter the Army at the age of 15. All he needed was a birth certificate that proved a birth year of 1930.

"I doctored up my birth certificate," he said. "I took bleach and took the '3' out. A railroad agent at Bemis, Brooks Good, was the station agent

Calvin Shifflett at his sales counter in Glady. Hikers passing through the crossroads relied upon the small store to replenish their supplies.

there, and he showed me how to do it. He lined up the certificate in the old typewriter and showed me how to make that a zero."

Calvin then made a photocopy of the doctored birth certificate, which the Army accepted without question. Assigned to the infantry, Calvin spent three years in the Army and completed his high school education during that time.

He came back to Randolph County after the service and, in 1953, married Frances Hedrick, a childhood friend from Bemis. They had seven children.

Calvin's Place

Calvin got a job at Metal Lab in Beverly, where he advanced to finishing supervisor. But the work took him all over the country, and he got tired of the travel.

In 1961, he built a little tavern in Bemis to supplement his factory income. The community had died in the early 1950s, when the last of the mines closed. Property was selling at bargain prices, and Calvin purchased one of the row houses, as well as the school. Many of the old buildings were being torn down, and there was a large supply of used lumber.

It was from this lumber that Calvin built the first room of his bar. "I

Calvin Shifflett was shopkeeper and bartender at his place in Bemis.

had the lot and a basement full of used lumber," he said. "I traded a heifer calf to a guy for a load of ¾-inch sheathing. The sides and roof of my first building, that's what I sheathed it with."

Calvin originally planned to build a venue for playing country music, but people started bringing in beer and he realized he'd soon find himself in trouble with the law if he didn't get a license. He was licensed in 1962 and never sold anything but beer because a liquor license required food service. Business boomed, and he put on two additions to serve the dozens of people who crowded into the bar on weekend evenings.

Calvin's Place served a mostly seasonal clientele, folks who owned seasonal cottages and campers in Bemis. He also had patrons who drove across Cheat Mountain from Beverly on a narrow gravel road to congregate in this homey pub. A wood-burning stove heated the space, and patrons contributed to their comfort by carrying in a log or two as needed. Grocery items were stocked behind the bar.

The most striking feature of this establishment were the 3,500 or so dollar bills taped to its ceiling and walls. Each bill was autographed by the person or party who contributed to this tradition. It dated to 1975, when

Calvin Shifflett's Place in Bemis. Nothing fancy, just a watering hole and store, but folks drove long distances over narrow, rutted roads to get there.

a couple of men from Charleston affixed their souvenir currency on the ceiling. Hundreds of patrons followed suit and left their mark on Bemis one buck at a time.

The donations include a bill signed by U.S. Representative Alan Mollohan and his wife on June 26, 1987. "Mollohan used to stop here quite

Hundreds of Calvin's bar patrons signed and attached to the ceiling and walls a dollar bill. Calvin never worried about someone stealing them because none of the bills cost him a dime.

a bit when he went bear hunting in these parts," Calvin said. Currency from several foreign countries and some bills larger than a greenback were mixed in with the prosaic bucks. "I had a $100-bill," Calvin said. "This guy wanted to beat his brother, so he put up a $100 bill. It took about two weeks before somebody stole it."

Well, kind of. They replaced it with a fifty.

Calvin didn't worry about patrons stealing the money or a fire claiming it all.

"I ain't cost me nothing," he said.

The Glady Post Office closed May 14, 2011. Even as Calvin's health failed, he continued to return to his store at Bemis to reconnect with his retail, bar, and postal patrons. His last visit was Memorial Day 2019; he died August 13.

It is debatable as to whether or not Peter Shaver was actually buried at this location between Glady and Alpena, but it is known that the pioneer, who was killed by Native Americans, was associated with the land. Calvin Shifflett cared for the memorial.

Along the Way: Peter Shaver's Burial Site

In addition to his duties as shopkeeper, bar owner, and assistant postmaster of Glady, Calvin Shifflett also was caretaker of Peter Shaver's burial site.

Located in a meadow off Randolph County Road 27 between Glady and Alpena, the grave was marked by an American flag, a large flat stone, and a modern stainless-steel marker bearing the inscription, "Here lies Peter Shaver killed by Indians 1781. This mountain and Shavers Fork River are named in his honor."

Calvin first erected a sign at the site in the 1970s. He drove by it on his way to work and one day noticed that the small sign erected by the Randolph County Historical Society was missing. He made a new sign at work, but it, too, was soon stolen.

"I made up signs and the hoodlums kept stealing them," he said. "I guess people would take them and put them in their den. It was a conversation piece to brag about, to say they had taken Peter Shaver's grave marker."

The stainless marker was the work of Jeff Darnell, who rented a cabin from Calvin. Jeff welded the marker to a 6-foot-steel barbed pole; he and Joe Horty drove the thing into the ground with sledgehammers. "No one has attempted to pull that one out," Calvin claimed. "They'd have to have a bulldozer to get it out."

Calvin's son-in-law, Terry Site of Belington, kept the little plot mowed. "Someone puts a flag up there, but I don't know who does that," Calvin said. "There's always a good-looking flag up there."

Calvin felt that it was important to honor the pioneer because of his contributions to settling the area. However, he said the site is more ceremonial than historical. Peter's body was probably interred elsewhere. The meadow is believed to have been the site of his cabin; a limestone spring near the burial site supports that placement. However, Homer Floyd Fansler's 1962 *History of Tucker County,* suggests the site was that of a ranger hut. Another author suggested that Shaver's cabin at Collette Gap was an outpost for hunting and refuge from the Shawnees; his cabin was elsewhere in the Tygart Valley.

Shaver was an Indian ranger and soldier in the Revolutionary War. He and his wife, Sarah, their three sons, and Shaver's sickly brother, Paul, lived

Calvin Shifflett attempted to discourage vandalism of Peter Shaver's grave by commissioning a metal marker that was deeply embedded in the ground.

on what is now Shaver Mountain in 1772. Indians scalped Peter Shaver and deposited his body across a path. Sarah and Paul discovered the bloody remains as they rode home from visiting other settlers. Horrified by the gruesome sight, Sarah, who was pregnant, put her hand to her face to hide it from her eyes.

"Her brother-in-law, Paul, tried to quiet her by saying it was a log across the trail, but it was apparent that he had been killed and scalped only a few minutes before," Fansler stated.

The Shaver family fled the area. Several months later, Sarah gave birth to a son, Francis, whose face bore a large red birthmark in the shape of a human hand. The mark was attributed to her reaction upon seeing Peter's mutilated body.

Calvin also maintained a private cemetery in the backyard at Bemis. Sited along the railroad tracks, the cemetery was for all the dogs Calvin and his wife owned over the years.

In all my wanderings, that little cemetery was one of the most poignant sights I ever saw. A year after visiting Calvin, I had to place my beloved golden retriever, Clifford, in my own little plot dedicated to our canine family members.

No matter where we live or wander, life moves too quickly for those who love both dogs and obscure places gone but not easily forgotten.

Chapter 8

The Punch Jones Diamond

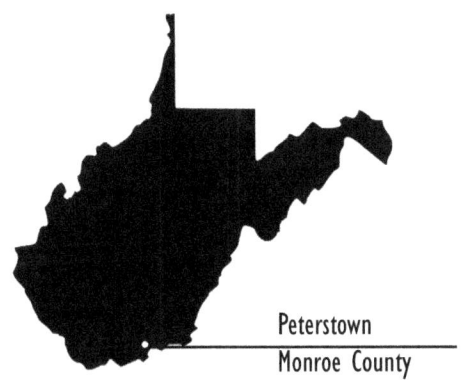

The odds are staggering: The couple who held the world record for the most consecutive male births (sixteen) also owned the Peterstown property on which was found the largest alluvial diamond ever discovered in the United States.

It was the firstborn of this brood, William P. "Punch" Jones, who discovered the gem. He and his father, Grover C. Jones, Sr., were pitching horseshoes in their yard in April 1928 when Punch noticed a piece of glass where the dirt had been disturbed. Fascinated by the stone, the 10-year-old boy decided to save it in a cigar box, which his father stashed in a tool shed on their property.

Grover and Annie Grace (Buckland) Jones lived in a modest, one-story frame house on Sycamore Street. The street dead ends at the house, or more accurately, Rich Creek, which borders the side yard, then cuts a course parallel to Sycamore before flowing under Route 219.

The tool shed where Punch stored his discovery was gone when I visited the family in 2007, but Charlotte Ann Faulkner, the Jones' sole daughter and number seventeen in the line, still lived in the family home and pointed

Punch Jones family, 1940. *West Virginia and Regional History Center at WVU.*

out where the shed stood. By the time she was born, 1946, the gem was on loan to the Smithsonian Institution in Washington, D.C., where it remained until 1964, when Grover requested its return.

Grover was born in Red Sulfur Springs on April 19, 1889. He and Annie Grace, who was 12 years his junior, met while Grover was teaching elementary school in Virginia. They were married on April 19, 1916.

Thus began the union that led to what is apparently the world's record for male consecutive births (Guinness had not tracked this accomplishment). Punch came along in 1917 and 15 more boys followed: Robert "Bay," Dick, Tom, John, Paul, Woodrow "Monk," Tad, Willard, Pete, Grover Jr. "June Bug," Rufus, Buck, Franklin Delano "Sam," Leslie "Arms" Howard (named after the famous actor) and Giles Monroe. Eleven of the 16 boys served in the military between World War II and the Korean War.

Evidently, the couple were having a difficult time coming up with male names by the time boy number sixteen arrived. Giles, born in January 1942, was known only as "Baby Jones" until March, when his birth certificate was amended to "Giles Monroe," the names of the adjoining West Virginia/Virginia counties where they lived.

There was no precedent on either side of the family for multiple consecutive male births, nor was the feat repeated in subsequent generations. Grover Junior had five consecutive girls, then a boy; another son fathered one boy and two girls.

Sixteen of them, all boys

For the first 30 years of Grover's and Annie Grace's marriage, girls were more scarce than diamonds in the Jones household.

"My mother used to joke with me," said Charlotte, who, as the only girl and youngest child, felt she enjoyed a very special relationship with her mother. "She'd say she never gave up on having a girl. We were real close; my mother and I were really close."

The large family and Grover's meager teacher's salary ensured a hardscrabble existence. "We had a rough time, I'll tell you," said Woodrow, who lived in Galion, Ohio. "It was rough, we had a rough time getting food."

Charlotte had a copy of her father's 1945 contract with the Giles County,

Virginia, School Board, which set his salary at $130 per month for nine months.

A garden, flock of chickens, and cow helped stretch the meager salary at the Jones's dinner table, and the boys recall the family having enough food to share with others. In the economy of that era and place, the Jones family was neither poorer nor richer than most of their neighbors. Their greatest assets were their determination and children, and as soon as Punch and the older boys were able to work outside the home, they did so to bring in extra income. Both Punch and Robert labored for the Works Progress Administration in the 1930s.

Grover entered the teaching profession with just an eighth-grade education, but as standards changed, he was forced to complete college courses to retain his job. He studied at Radford College in the summers of 1913 to 1917 and from 1932 to 1936. He never obtained a college degree, yet Hazel Overstreet, Punch's widow and a resident of Chesapeake, Virginia, said her late father-in-law called himself "Professor Grover Jones, Esquire."

Annie Grace did not work outside the home, nor would it have been practical with at least a half dozen youngsters under her care during a span of almost three decades. The boys recalled their home as having four bedrooms, and Woodrow said it was common to sleep five boys to a bed.

With that many mouths to feed, meals tended to last all day. As for discipline, much of the responsibility for oversight fell upon the older boys, especially Punch, who served as a mentor and example of good behavior. Neither Grover nor Annie Grace had time to dote on one child, and the boys learned to "dry up" whenever they started bellyaching.

The Jones boys were good athletes, and they could usually stay out of trouble by finding a touch football game to occupy their time. The men recalled their father as an excellent fiddler, and on Friday evenings Grover joined other string players in the "Lower Room" of the Jones home for a community square dance. James Buckland, Grover's father-in-law, called the dances. Looking back on those days, Woodrow found it amazing that so many people squeezed into that room and still found space to dance.

In 1940 the family of 15 boys and their parents were thrust into the national spotlight. The occasion was the World's Fair in New York. A millionaire paid the family's train fare for a round-trip from Bluefield to New York City, where they were put on public display through personal appearances and radio and print interviews. October 3, 1940, was declared "Grover Jones Family Day" at the World's Fair.

Woodrow, 15 at the time, recalled two highlights from the experience. Each child received a set of new clothes, paid for by the sponsor. "First time in my life," he said of the new threads. His other memory is of meeting Judy Garland and Mickey Rooney, who were filming *Strike Up the Band* in New York at the time.

The six-day trip included appearances on national radio programs and a visit to the White House, where they were to meet President Franklin Delano Roosevelt. The president was unavailable, and the first lady received them.

Carnation Milk Company offered Grover and Annie Grace a publicity/endorsement deal that would have generated extra income to raise their standard of living and make life much easier. Woodrow Jones told me that his father declined.

"My mother and dad were private people," Charlotte said. "They liked their privacy."

Sudden wealth

The family returned to Peterstown and their hardscrabble lives. One more boy was born to them, then the sole girl. Punch followed in his father's footsteps, went away to college, and became a teacher. After the Radford Arsenal was built in nearby Radford, Virginia, Punch exchanged teaching for defense work.

While working at the ammunitions factory, Punch learned about the various forms of carbon, an ingredient of gunpowder. He got to thinking about the sparkling stone he'd found fourteen years earlier and decided to ask Dr. Roy Holden, a geology professor at Virginia Polytechnic Institute and State University at Blacksburg, to look at his childhood treasure.

As a geologist, Holden frequently was approached by people who thought they had found a diamond when, in fact, it was a chunk of quartz. He suspected Punch Jones' stone would be no different. "It just looked like a piece of glass to me," said Hazel Overstreet, recalling the first time Punch showed it to her.

One look at the 5/8-inch, 34.48-carat, bluish-white, 12-faced diamond

Charlotte Ann Jones Faulkner stands in the yard of her parents' home and points to area where the horseshoe pit was located. It was there that the Punch Jones Diamond, the largest alluvial diamond found in the United States, was noticed by her brother in April 1923. Of the 17 children born to Grover and Annie Grace Jones, Charlotte was the only girl. Photo from 2008.

that Punch pulled from his pocket changed Holden's gaze from boredom to amazement. It was the largest alluvial diamond ever discovered in the United States.

Alluvial diamonds are found away from the igneous rock deposits that bear diamonds from deep within the earth. Alluvials are usually found in river gravels that carry the stones away from their original source. Rich Creek, which periodically overflowed its banks onto the Jones property, was thus credited as the conduit for this incredibly rare find.

Some locals had other origination theories, suggesting that a bird found the diamond and fortuitously dropped it on the Jones' property. Others thought it originated in a pile of coal near the horseshoe court; some suggested it fell to earth from outer space. Regardless of how it got there, its validation as a gem brought prospectors to Rich Creek hoping finding its sister in the creek's gravel bottom.

"People have come by wanting to look around," Charlotte said. "They just wanted to walk up on a diamond . . . It would be nice if another one would come by."

Hazel, who had dated Punch since high school, told me that Punch was soon separated from his fortune after the gem was verified. Punch was drafted, and, following up on Holden's suggestion, he placed the gem in the care of the Smithsonian Institution in Washington, D.C., until he could return from the war and decide what to do with it.

Although his induction into the Army accelerated their relationship, Hazel said Punch did not offer to make an engagement ring from the diamond. "He didn't know what to do with it right then," Hazel said.

One of Punch's younger brothers drove Hazel to Tyler, Texas, where she and Punch were married July 26, 1943, in the home of a preacher. Punch, who was in training to be a pilot, moved on to Colorado, then Missouri, at which point Hazel returned to West Virginia to live.

In December 1944, while Punch was on leave, Hazel gave birth to their son, Robert. Hazel said her husband's leave was cut short by a massive call for reinforcements to assist the Allied effort at the Battle of the Bulge. The Battle of the Bulge forced him out of the pilot-training program and into the 97th Infantry. He had only three days to spend with his new son.

That Christmas holiday was the last time Hazel and the Jones family saw Punch alive. Hazel said her late husband was extremely emotional as he departed, almost as if he had a premonition of his fate.

While in California awaiting deployment overseas, he made a recording and sent it to his son to listen to at some future date. "He told Bob to be good to me because I'm a real good person," Hazel said. But he made no mention of the diamond.

String of tragedies

Punch's luck ran out April 1, Easter Sunday, 1945, while conducting patrol operations in Belgium. The patrol of 10 to 12 men of the 97th Infantry came under attack, most likely from German resistance; only two survived to tell of it. Punch was not one of them.

Woodrow, a tank operator, was involved in his own struggle for life just nine miles away on the Rhine River when Punch was killed. Six months passed before he learned that his brother was dead. Punch was buried in

The historical marker along Route 219 is near the creek that is suspected of having delivered the alluvial diamond to the Jones' property. The diamond was eventually sold to a buyer in the Orient.

Belgium. His remains were returned to the United States in 1950 and laid to rest in the Peterstown Cemetery.

The sight of a War Department telegram was familiar to Grover and Annie Grace. In June 1944, their son Paul was shot in the leg six days after hitting Omaha Beach. He recuperated at a hospital in England, then went back to the front, only to be shot in the same leg again. Another son, Robert, became seriously ill while serving with the Navy in Italy. Woodrow was shot in the hand while exiting his tank.

Hazel said Punch had made a will, which gave 50 percent joint ownership of the ring to her and their children, and 50 percent to his parents. But Punch's death put the diamond in a new light for the family; its sentimental value meant more to Grover than its monetary worth, and he refused to sell it.

The gem, which became known as the Punch Jones Diamond, remained in The Smithsonian's custody.

Russell Feather, museum specialist-gemologist with the Smithsonian in Washington, D.C., recalled a brief conversation he had with Dr. Ed Henderson, curator of the gem, back in the mid-1980s.

"He recalled that the Jones family did not want anyone handling the diamond at all," recalled Feather. "He told them if Mrs. Roosevelt wanted to handle the stone that he would let her."

Most of the Jones children grew up never seeing the diamond that bore the family name.

"The first time I ever saw it was when I graduated in 1964 and we went on a senior trip to Washington, D.C., and I saw it in the Smithsonian," Charlotte said.

Later that year, the diamond was returned to Grover Sr., who placed it in a safety deposit box in the First Valley National Bank, Rich Creek, Virginia. Its lone public appearance in West Virginia was during a State Fair in Lewisburg.

Hazel attempted to get custody of the diamond so she could sell it and raise cash to help her son with college expenses. The effort ended in court when Grover Sr. refused to acknowledge her claim. Robert Jones, son of Punch and Hazel, told me the judge ruled that Grover and Annie Grace had a 75-percent claim to the stone, largely because the gem was discovered on their property. Robert's claim was only 25 percent, and Hazel had no claim. Grover, increasingly sentimental about the gem, refused to sell. Long-standing animosity between Hazel and Grover, arising from Hazel's decision to move away from West Virginia after Punch died, also figured into the standoff, Robert said.

Grover died in 1976 at the age of 84. In 1984, Robert and Annie Grace came to an agreement to sell the diamond through Southeby's Auction House in New York. It sold for $67,500, which left them with $60,750 after commission. Robert bore additional sales expenses from his share, as well as expenses that his grandmother had accumulated in a previous attempt to sell the gem. The diamond went to a buyer in the Orient, and the family lost track of it at that point.

Robert said his motivation for selling the diamond was to raise cash to help his grandmother in her senior years. He was certain that his father would have wanted it that way. Ideally, Robert wished the diamond could have stayed in the Smithsonian.

"I think the diamond was for (Punch) probably a lot like it was for me,"

Robert told me. "It was important to me that he was the one who found it and it had some significant value in the history of West Virginia, and it was there to help take care of my grandmother if she needed it."

Annie Grace died in 1992. Although some newspaper reports quoted her as saying she wished Punch and Grover had never found the diamond and would just "throw it in the New River," Charlotte said her mother never expressed those sentiments to her. Nor did her parents ever sense that the diamond brought bad luck, despite Punch's tragic death.

Indeed, for the most part, the family simply ignored the diamond.

"We never thought too much about the diamond," Woodrow said. "We never thought it was worth anything."

"It was just one of those things that, after the novelty wore off, it was taken for granted," Charlotte said. "I think my father and mother just chose to do it that way. They were not greedy people in any sense of the word. They were very satisfied with the life they lived."

Along the Way: Chenoweth Covered Bridges

The double-barrel covered bridge at Philippi is a reconstruction of the original bridge built by Lemuel Chenoweth of Beverly. Chenoweth built several covered bridges on the western Virginia turnpikes that are now part of West Virginia's highway system.

West Virginia's longest covered bridge is also one of the nation's few surviving double-barrel covered bridges. It is 285 ½ feet long, slightly shorter than its original 312 feet when built in 1852 by famed, self-taught Appalachian bridge builder Lemuel Chenoweth.

The Randolph County resident and his brother Eli constructed 20 bridges on four western-Virginia turnpikes. Chenoweth made extensive use of the Burr-arch truss design, which was a significant improvement over the simple truss designs of earlier wooden bridges. Chenoweth (1811-1887) also was a carpenter and legislator. He built his home in Beverly and the Huttonsville Presbyterian Church in Huttonsville, both of which are extant. The post-and-beam home houses a museum that honors the life of this master bridge builder whose Philippi creation still carries vehicular traffic, albeit with significant reinforcement.

Lemuel Chenoweth's other extant West Virginia covered bridge is at Barrackville. The bridge has been bypassed, but pedestrians can use it.

The Philippi bridge crosses the Tygart Valley River as part of US Route 250 (Beverly-Fairmont Turnpike) and is the only covered bridge on a national numbered highway. Using the Burr-arch truss design, the bridge cost $12,180.68 when constructed.

Less than a decade after completion, it was the site of what some historians consider the first land battle of the American Civil War. The clash between Confederate and Union forces has been dubbed the "Philippi Races" because of the pace at which the Confederates high-tailed it out of the town. The Union soldiers captured the bridge and pressed it into service as barracks.

Less than two years later, at a time when Confederates were conducting raids on the B&O Railroad, orders were issued to burn covered bridges in the region. The structure escaped destruction thanks to pleading by Southern sympathizers. However, on February 2, 1989, an unfortunate chain of events did what neither army nor flooding succeeded at accomplishing. Gasoline spilled from a nearby filling station whose bulk tank was being filled, and the fuel flowed onto the bridge. The exhaust system

Lemuel Chenoweth made extensive use of the Burr arch design for his wooden truss bridges. This example is found in the Barrackville Bridge.

of a car that was crossing the bridge backfired, and the old bridge became a conflagration of history.

Virtually destroyed by the fire, the old bridge was replaced by a new one whose exterior was painstakingly modeled after the original. The reconstruction was completed in 1991 and cost $1.4 million.

The project equipped historians, the state, and contractors with the knowledge to tackle restoration of the state's remaining covered bridges. The Barrackville Bridge, also built by Chenoweth, was restored in the late 1990s. Rotted truss members and the roof were replaced and a wooden floor system installed in accordance with the bridge's original 1853 design. Originally constructed without siding, the bridge was given a bright red exterior during the nearly $1.5-million project.

Barrackville carries only pedestrian traffic (a new bridge for motorized traffic bypasses it), making it a good destination for wandering about a bridge interior without fear of being mowed down by a vehicle.

Dorsey Wiseman speaks to the audience during the 2004 Singing in the Hills gathering on the Wiseman property in Mabie. Although his face was disfigured from surgeries to remove the bone cancer and his fingers could not longer pluck the strings in his guitar because of nerve damage caused by chemotherapy, Dorsey gave a testimony of grace and healing at the hands of God. His music reflected this same spirit of gratitude and faith. Dorsey Wiseman lived his faith, regardless of his circumstances.

Chapter 9

The Wiseman of Mabie

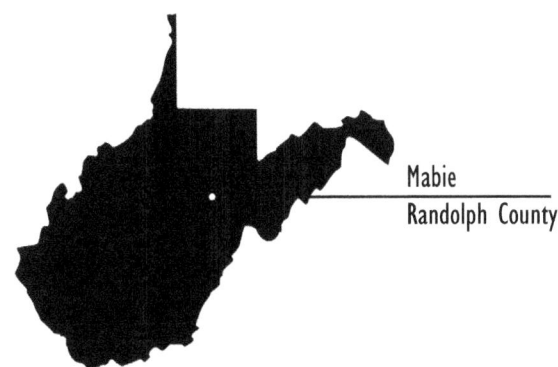

Mabie
Randolph County

Dorsey Wiseman was walking through the Meadowbrook Mall in Clarksburg when he heard a female pianist playing a familiar tune outside a jewelry store. He approached her after she'd finished playing and asked if she knew the song's name.

She had no idea, but said she loved the music.

Dorsey proceeded to tell her that she had just played the "Lonesome Fiddle Waltz" and she was talking to its composer.

In the 1960s, this Mabie, Randolph County, native began penning tunes that permeate the repertoire of many Mountain State gospel and country singers. Bridgeport musician John Graham frequently sang Dorsey's composition "When I Count My Blessings, The Best One is You," a song Dorsey wrote to honor his wife, Harriet. Sutton daughter-mother duo Carolyn Connor and Missy Connor Scarbro performed several of Dorsey's tunes at their concerts, including his signature song "The Beacon," recorded by the Marvin Clark Family on their 2003 *In Times Like These* release. Several other groups expressed an interest in recording more of his gospel music.

Dorsey's music also was played and celebrated at the annual "Singing

Dorsey Wiseman outside the Harrison Community Church, which stands where Dorsey's grandmother once had her garden. The church grounds hosts Singing in the Hills. Photograph from September 2003.

in the Hills," which he started in 1974. The weekend gospel sing is held the second full weekend in August in the pavilion at Harrison Community Church, which rises on a hill above the modest, white block house where Dorsey and Harriet lived.

I met them at that home in September 2003. As he gave me a tour of his property and neighborhood, Dorsey told me that his family donated the land for the church, which stands where his grandmother had her garden. His father and neighbors collected donations to purchase construction materials for the church, which they finished in 1957. It was paid in full when they drove the last nail in the building and had remained as such ever since.

"It has never owed five cents to anybody," he said of the independent congregation.

The community of Mabie, Randolph County, is imbued with memories and Wiseman history going back to 1916. Dorsey was born October 13, 1937, in Grafton. His parents, Ben and Lanora, moved back to the Wiseman homestead in Mabie when Dorsey was a year old. The home of his paternal grandparents, Garrett and Birdie Wiseman, stood on the hill above his house, which his father built in 1943. Dorsey's father cleared the land around and behind the house for pasture.

Ben Wiseman spent thirty-five years in coal mines, then finished out his working days as a state highway employee. "He got into a bees' nest while working, got stung, and had two heart attacks," Dorsey said.

The youngest of four children, Dorsey sang as soon as he started talking.

"I can't remember a time when I wasn't singing," he said. "My mother was the main reason for that. She taught all of us how to sing, and I've been singing all my life. All my life, I've known nothing but music."

He also credited his mother for making him and his sisters—Lena, June and Margaret—comfortable in front of a microphone.

"My mother would set a broom in front of us like a microphone stand, and that's how we got started," he said.

"We sang in churches ever since he was 5 or 6," said sister Lena Wiseman Simmons, who lived down the road from her brother. "He'd be out playing in the dirt, and we'd have to go and get him and bring him in. He'd sing in his dirty feet."

In addition to finding his knack for making music on Rich Mountain, Dorsey found a spiritual rock in Mabie's Methodist Church. "We would walk from here to the church every morning, walk back home, and walk to church and back again every Sunday night. I've been living for the Lord ever since I was 6 or 7 years old. It's paid off for me," Dorsey said.

Like many other budding Appalachian musicians of the 1940s, Dorsey was inspired by the "old-timer" musicians who lived in the community. Further inspiration came from his mother, the church pianist.

"Everybody on the mountain here played music of some kind," he said. "You just watched it to learn."

Saturday-night radio broadcasts of the Grand Ole Opry and regional gospel singers provided additional exposure and inspiration.

"I used to listen to Hank Williams' songs, the Sons of the Pioneers, western music," he said. He also listened to "Little" John Graham and Cherokee Sue on WMMN, Fairmont, although he and Graham would not meet personally until the early 1990s at the School of Hard Knocks.

Dorsey chose the guitar as his instrument. Lena said the family's first guitar was one that their mother obtained while cleaning out her mother-in-law's house. "They had this guitar, and they couldn't learn to play it, so they gave it to my mother," Lena said.

Lena learned to play the instrument and accompanied Dorsey on it. And Dorsey played it until he could afford his own instrument. That opportunity came while he was a sophomore at Coalton High School.

"My father gave me a calf and I raised it to a baby beef that could be sold at auction," Dorsey said. "I got $129.50 out of it. I bought a Gibson guitar off Keys' Music in Elkins. It was $139. I lacked $10, and they trusted me for it. The next year, I raised another calf, but I got only $29 for it. Truman was president when I raised the first one, then Eisenhower got in the next year and there was a big drop in the price of meat."

Owning his own guitar provided Dorsey with a ticket to perform. He sang in churches, schools, and on WDNE in Elkins. "I don't remember when I first sang on WDNE, but I was young, young, young," he said.

Lena said her brother possessed a voice like that of Mac Wiseman, although the family claims no kinship to the famous bluegrass singer.

"(Dorsey) was a good singer, he sure was," recalled Mary Martin of Richmond, Virginia, who grew up at Mill Creek and recalled hearing Dorsey sing with the Watson siblings at her church. She believed that Dorsey could have gone professional if he tried. However, despite his success in the Elkins music scene, Dorsey enlisted in the US Army just two weeks after high school graduation in 1956.

He ended up at Fort Knox, Kentucky, where he quickly made friends with two other musicians, mandolin player Chuck Elmore and upright bass player Dave Brown. They formed the Fort Knox Trio and played bluegrass at venues on the post, at the Lincoln Jamboree at Hodginsville, Kentucky, and the Kentucky Jamboree.

Dorsey recalled each member receiving $20 from the gigs. "I drew $65 a month Army pay and I made $80 a month playing music," he said. The trio spent a year together, then disbanded when Dave Brown headed back to North Carolina and Elmore got in trouble for wrecking the general's new automobile.

The trio emulated the Osborne Brothers' style and content. Dorsey was not writing his own songs at that time; the muse came after he was discharged. He came back to Mabie and tried to scratch out a living building wooden cabinets at a Beverly factory.

He teamed up with two other local musicians, Jimmy and Loren "Lodi" Currence of Cassity, who found a spot on WBOY television in Clarksburg. They had a twice-weekly bluegrass show and personal appearances in theaters and events. "In my opinion, the Currence Brothers was the best bluegrass band there's been around here in a long time," Dorsey recalled.

Dorsey began writing his own material about this time. His first song, "To Vietnam," was recorded by the Currence Brothers. Other early songs included "Roll On, You Lonesome Train" and "Big Sandy." He also teamed up with Pee Wee Heckel, Charlie Skidmore, and Boyd Phillips to form the Hometown Boys. The group played country and gospel tunes and had a program on WDNE.

"They'd put us on there about any time," Dorsey said.

Ohio beckons

In 1959, Dorsey married Harriet George, who was given the nickname of "Tippie" in childhood because she walked on her tiptoes. The couple had four children—daughters Kimberly Underwood and Cheryl Town, sons Timothy and Benjamin. Dorsey's $1.05-an-hour salary at the factory and moonlighting income from singing couldn't provide all the family's needs. "You couldn't make a living on that, you just couldn't make it," he said.

Dorsey was doing well enough in music that he could have gone on the road with it, but he was not interested in leaving his family. "I had a choice to make: Go into music big time or stay at home and take care of my wife and children," he said. "I felt I owed it to my family to stay home and raise my children."

Like many young West Virginians of his generation, Dorsey followed the path north to the factories of northeast Ohio in search of better pay. In the late 1950s, his sisters and their husbands, June and Howard Watson and Margaret and Ellis Gilmore, headed north to work at Packard

Dorsey Wiseman raised a calf to make the money to purchase his first guitar. He stands with his favorite one outside his home in Mabie, September 2003.

Electric in Warren. Dorsey and Harriet followed their trail in March 1964, immediately after Dorsey finished his commitment to the Army Reserve. In Ohio, Dorsey found work as a welder and layout man for a structural steel company.

"Four dollars an hour," he said. "That was big money compared to what I got in West Virginia."

Dorsey's faith and music converged in Ohio, where he wrote divinely inspired songs. "I'm really not the writer, I'm just the penman," he said of his sacred compositions. He teamed up with his sisters June and Margaret to make his first album, *The Wisemans: Sounds of Home* (Marbone Records). The album contained two of Dorsey's original songs, the title cut and "My Cup Runneth over with His Love."

In the 1960s and 1970s, Northeast Ohio became a hotbed of country and bluegrass music as Appalachian migrants reconstituted their displaced communities around the fiddle, banjo, Dobro, and mandolin. Dorsey worked with a number of these mountain-rooted bluegrass groups in the region, including the Butler Brothers, Family Pride, and the West Virginia

Many young West Virginia-born men and their wives migrated to the Warren, Ohio, area to take advantage of the relatively high paying jobs. These migrants brought their music north with them and started bluegrass and gospel groups. An annual gathering of them was held in the Ravenna, Ohio, barn of Titus and Dolores Shifflett. Photo from November 2003 gathering.

Travelers—the bluegrass band of Sutton native John Douglas (father of 14-time Grammy winner Jerry Douglas).

"I really think we took the mountain music right along with us," Dorsey said. "The people from Tennessee were there, and the people from Kentucky were there."

Like many of the Appalachian migrants, Dorsey frequently made the eight-hour trek back to his mountain home on weekends, vacations, and holidays. While on one of those trips Dorsey received the inspiration to start Singing in the Hills. The instructions came while he was sitting in the pavilion of the Harrison Community Church.

"God told me to have it," he said. "He put it in my heart to have a sing there. God said, 'Here is where I want you to start it.'"

Years later, Dorsey heard from God again, an answer to a prayer he'd breathed several weeks earlier while driving on the Ohio Turnpike near his home in Warren.

"I asked God, 'What can I do for you?' Three weeks later he woke me up at 3 a.m. and in a voice as clear as me talking to you now, he said, 'I know your heart, you're not after money and not after fame. I'll open the doors and make the way.'"

Two weeks later, an acquaintance from a gospel group called Dorsey and asked him to come to Nashville to meet with two other groups that wanted him to write songs for them. Confident that God had opened the door to a new career, Dorsey went to Nashville, but he changed his mind once he saw the lifestyle entertainers lived. There would be too many concessions, too many compromises with his faith, and he declined the offer.

"I could have made it big in Nashville, but I walked out," he said. "I knew it wasn't what God wanted me to do, and I haven't been back. Money don't mean nothing to me."

He suffered a string of lay-offs that left him discouraged and tired. "Eight places shut down on me," he said. "The last one, the (new owners) came in and took the dies right off the machine I was working on. They laid us off and took all our jobs and moved them Mexico. I said I might as well go back home and take care of Mom and Dad."

Hard times followed them back to Mabie when they arrived there in the spring of 1993. While working at a sawmill, a grinding wheel blew apart and cut through nerves, muscles, and veins in Dorsey's left leg near the groin. A long, painful recovery followed.

Borrowed Time

Three years later, in September 1996, Dorsey was involved in a traffic crash with a tractor-trailer rig that demolished his vehicle. Thanks to the seat belts they were wearing, Dorsey and his passenger, granddaughter Elizabeth Barron, survived. But less than two months after the accident, Dorsey discovered a lump on his rib cage where the seat belt impacted his body.

The lump turned out to be multiple myeloma, an aggressive, fatal cancer of the bone marrow. He sought treatment at the Cleveland Clinic, where doctors gave him a poor prognosis. His only hope was an experimental

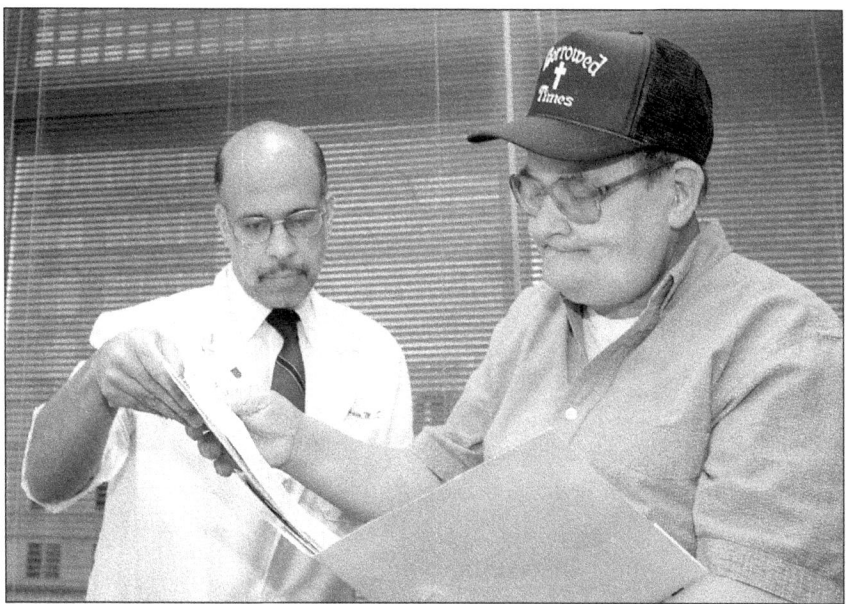

Dr. Mohammed Hussein, Dorsey Wiseman's cancer specialist, reviews his blood work during a visit to the Cleveland Clinic, where he was the hospital's longest-surviving bone cancer patient and underwent experimental therapies. Dorsey used his times in the cancer ward to share God's love with others going through the horrible disease.

treatment, which Dorsey agreed to try. Dorsey underwent twenty-one months of chemotherapy. Partway through the treatment, doctors discovered that the drug was damaging his heart, and Dorsey required bypass surgery for five blockages.

He went into remission, but the cancer came back with vengeance. At one point in 2001, he had cancer in eighty-five percent of his bone marrow and his kidneys had shut down. The doctor told his wife to make funeral and burial arrangements. But Dorsey believed God had something else for him to do.

"I went into complete remission," he said.

The cancer returned, this time in his jaw. Doctors removed his left jawbone and, in the spring of 2003, fashioned a new one using a bone from his lower leg. "They wrote on my hospital chart that I have a deformed jaw," he said. "But I don't have a deformed jaw, I have a reformed jaw. I used to put my foot in my mouth, now I got my whole leg in there."

Dorsey Wiseman with one of his musician friends, John Graham of Bridgeport, during the 2004 Singing in the Hills. The event was both a celebration in music and homecoming for the friends and musicians of Dorsey Wiseman. See *Still More Wandering Back-Roads West Virginia (Volume IX)* for stories about Singing in the Hills and John Graham/Sagebrush Roundup.

The cancer returned with full force in the summer of 2004; Dorsey drew nigh to death's door. Another experimental treatment and round of fervent prayers from Christians across the nation brought healing to Dorsey, just in time for him to preside at the thirtieth anniversary of Singing in the Hills.

"We've been here praying for him, and God's really been touching him," said Dorsey's friend and prayer partner from Coalton, Jerry Marco. "God's got a job for him to do, he's a good witness for the Lord."

Dorsey beat bone cancer for an incredible eight years, a feat that amazed his oncologist Dr. Mohammed A. Hussein of the Cleveland Clinic. But the chemotherapy destroyed the feeling in his fingers; he could no longer play the guitar. It also destroyed most of his hearing.

"My hearing keeps going down and down," Dorsey said. "But they can't take the music out of my mind."

Dorsey wore a black ball cap bearing the words "Borrowed Time." He used it as an opener to tell people about how God spared his life so he could carry on a ministry of comfort and encouragement to other cancer patients. During one of his ten-day stays in the clinic, Dorsey held a revival in the cancer ward as he visited and uplifted patients in the final stage of their battle.

"I got a greater ministry than I had before, working in a hospital, talking to people," he said. "I know what it's like to sit there and have them tell you that you only got three months to live. I know all about it. But where there is life, there is hope, and you better be knowing the Great Physician to take care of you.

"Now God's got me out of the music business, and he's got me into testifying," Dorsey added, summing up how that prayer on the Ohio Turnpike was answered. "But the music is still a big part of my life."

Dorsey and Tippie made more than one hundred trips from Mabie to the Cleveland Clinic during their battle with cancer. The travel, chemotherapy, and complications prevented Dorsey from writing songs for eight years. When we last talked in 2005, Dorsey was working with musicians like Marvin Clark to get his songs on paper and perhaps write a few new ones based upon his many trials.

One song in particular was rolling around his mind.

"I'm going to call it 'The Mountain Lullaby,'" he said. "I got a determination in my mind I'm going to write that song and finish it. And when I get it done, it will be a pretty song."

Dorsey Edward Wiseman died July 26, 2007, at the Cleveland Clinic from complications related to the bone cancer and treatment. It is believed he was the longest-surviving bone cancer patient in the United States at that time His wife died May 25, 2002.

Dorsey Wiseman (left) lived for the annual Singing in the Hills gathering, which he said God told him to start. Held on the Harrison Community Church grounds, the event drew musicians from as far away as Georgia for three days of singing and fellowship.

Along the Way: Filling Your Tank in Mabie

Since 1974, the second full weekend in August has been a time of gathering and praise at the Harrison Community Church in Mabie.

A revival, music festival, homecoming, and Sunday dinner on the grounds rolled into one event, Singing in the Hills grew to a three-day event (Friday, Saturday, Sunday) that has been condensed to a Saturday gathering in recent years.

Dorsey compared Singing in the Hills to pulling into a gas station and having your tank filled. "You just want to keep on going after that," he said. From the event's inception, Dorsey served as master of ceremonies. Between performances, he shared stories of his childhood, his love for God and gospel music, and his numerous miraculous recoveries from injuries and aggressive cancer.

Each performer was provided thirty minutes or so on stage—a slightly elevated area at the front of a metal pavilion. The audience spilled out of the pavilion, into the woods, and onto the grassy grounds surrounding the shelter.

While the hat was passed and the resulting collection shared among performers, there was no guarantee of compensation. That didn't discourage the artists from traveling long distances to participate.

"We just like it up here on the mountain," said Jerry Pryde, a gospel singer/evangelist who drove nearly 500 miles from Ontario, Canada, to be a part of the sing. "I worked in the South years ago, when I was in the music industry, and we just like it. It's a whole different atmosphere from at home. It's totally relaxed here."

Gospel singer Tommy Huff of Winder, Georgia, drove his motor home 537 miles to be a part of the family reunion in 2004.

"It's the people here," he said, explaining why he made the sacrifice of time and money. "The singers are not in competition with each other. We're here for the same purpose, for people to be saved and go to heaven. It ain't a money thing. It's a love-the-Lord thing and help-each-other thing."

"It's like a family reunion," said Coalton resident Jerry Marco. "It's like a homecoming, so many people have been coming here for so many years."

Friends and family of Dorsey Wiseman told me that Singing in the

Dorsey Wiseman is greeted by friends at the 2004 Singing in the Hills weekend on the Wiseman/Harrison Community Church grounds, Mabie.

Hills inspired Dorsey to courageously fight bone cancer for another year. "He lives for this from year to year," said Lena Simmons, his sister. "That's his big thing."

"There is singing, shouting and praising the Lord here on the mountain," Dorsey told me during the 2004 event. "God is here. He has not failed to witness himself to us. You go away from this place with your tank filled up."

The 49th annual Singing in the Hills was held August 14, 2023, according to the group's Facebook page, which provides updates on the Mabie tradition.

Chapter 10

Railroad Cross-ing in Belington

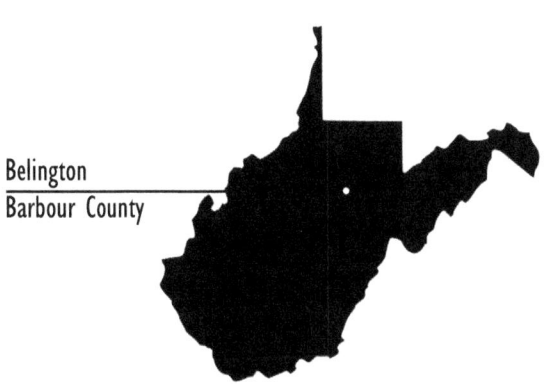

Dressed in his dark-blue outfit bedecked with bronze buttons and gold badges, Leon Dixon Cross looked like a railroad official who'd just walked out of an O. Winston Link photograph and into the Belington rail yard.

Leon, who was born March 24, 1938, was a fixture at the ticket office of the New Tygart Flyer, an excursion train on the former Western Maryland line. Leon walked a mile from his home to the ticket office each day that the train operated. He arrived three hours before it left the station so he also could serve as signal man when the engine rolled into the yard.

"Every morning I get up at 4 o'clock and go to work. I volunteer my time out here," he told me as we awaited the train's arrival on a Thursday morning in late September 2008. "I've been a security officer for them for I can't remember how long. I volunteer my time even though I got a broken hip, two broken bones in my wrist. They ain't going to keep me down."

Shirley Payne, one of Leon's sisters, said Leon wrecked his bicycle while he was riding home from working at the train station one afternoon. After

Leon Cross on the job. Belington, 2008.

that incident, he had to walk to the job that he loved more than anything else in the world.

Leon contracted rheumatic fever as a child, which led to multiple disabilities that vexed him throughout life. But he compensated for any disabilities with dedication and enthusiasm for his symbolic task. "I welcome people on the train and welcome them when they get off," he said. "I tell them how much we appreciate their riding with us."

He wore a jacket with "SECURITY" emblazoned across the back, a security guard's blue cap, a dark blue shirt and tie, blue pants, and a black conductor's vest from the New Jersey Railroad. A shiny security badge completed his uniform, which he wore with dedication and pride.

"I'm tickled to death to wear that. When you put those badges on, you're supposed to stick by it," he told me.

Leon carried a pair of handcuffs in his pocket but never used them. He was especially keen on protecting underage passengers and the United States of America. "I stand up for little kids and the American flag of the United States," he said. "If I have to, I'll go to prison to protect them."

Leon would not tolerate drinking, smoking, or foul talk on the train, especially in the presence of children. "This guy came on the train with a bus trip, and he was telling a filthy joke," Leon said. "I waited for him to finish telling the joke, then I arrested him. I was just kidding, but he sure got a kick out of that."

Leon was on duty throughout the six-hour, round-trip excursion to the High Falls of Cheat. He answered passengers' questions, gave them tips on the best side of the coaches to sit on for viewing the Shaver's Fork River scenery, and spun railroading stories from his childhood.

His father, the late Tas Cross, worked for Western Maryland for years. Leon followed his father to work at a young age.

"I'll tell you the truth . . . they weren't going to make no sissy out of me," he said. "I'd carry water to the men working on the track and they'd give me a penny."

Leon's young railroading career came to an abrupt halt when he was caught releasing the brakes on rail cars. "They got them stopped, but they didn't let me play on the railroad no more," he said.

As Leon got stronger and his misdeeds were forgotten, he worked for firemen who paid area boys to shovel the slag out of the steam locomotives' fireboxes. "As long as we were willing to do it, he'd give us a dollar a day," Leon said. "I thought I was a big spender."

Leon worked in a sawmill after completing eighth grade, which marked the end of his formal education.

"I've worked in just about everything: Forestry service, sawmills, everything. I ain't had no easy life," he said.

His work with the excursion line was through Red Payne, a stockholder. Leon helped pull weeds, clear overgrowth, and move railroad ties as the new owners readied the boarding site. He felt he was thus honoring the industry that gave livelihood to his family for more than four decades. And railroading also enriched the final decade of Leon's life.

"I'm going to tell you the truth," Leon said as he boarded the train. "This is what keeps me going. If I sat at home, I might not be able to walk today. This is what keeps me going."

Leon Dixon Cross died March 30, 2016, at the age of 78.

The Durbin and Greenbrier Valley Railroad operates its New Tygart Flyer out of Elkins. Visit https://mountainrailwv.com/ for excursion options and departure times.

T.S. Stobart takes a cigarette break outside his Paradox book store in Wheeling, March 2010. The oldest bookstore in West Virginia, Paradox was started by Stobart, a playwright and actor.

Chapter 11

Wheeling's Paradox

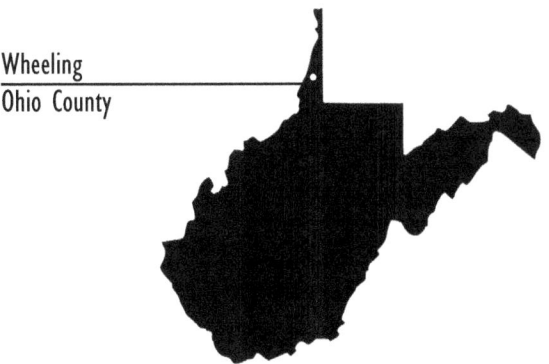

Thomas Scott Stobart's Paradox Bookstore in Wheeling took the concept of "independent bookseller to a whole new level. Stobart was so independent, neither he nor his store had an online presence.

"I loathe computers. I am a steampunk, a Luddite," Tom told me during our visit in March 2010.

"Steampunk" refers to a fantasy world where the age of steam co-exists with the age of technology; Luddite was a class of British textile workers who protested the industrial revolution, sometimes by destroying the mechanized looms.

Tom foresaw the same thing happening in the 21st century, but in reverse. "I think computers are destroying society," he said.

His disdain for technology was expressed on a succinct description printed on the gray bookmarks that doubled as business cards: "no 'phone, no Fax, no E-mail, irregular hours, indifferent service, inexplicable categorization, narrow aisles, murky lighting, breath-taking selection, dumbfounding prices, and NO DAMN CAT!"

T.S. Stobart chats with Harold Gene Vitalie, one of the shops frequent shoppers.

"I like to send telegrams. I like dial telephones. And I still write letters, although nobody ever writes back to me," Tom said.

He would have composed those letters on a typewriter, but his Olivetti broke, and Tom unsuccessfully searched for a replacement.

With embarrassment, he admitted to owning a VCR, but only to watch Marx Brothers films. He also (finally) acquired a cell phone, a purely financial decision because it was costing him so much to call 4-1-1 to find out who had called his land-line phone. Tom listened to books on tape while doing dishes, but cassette tape only. "No CD player," said Tom, who preferred to extract his music from vinyl grooves.

Tom admitted to committing a great infraction to his character, comparable to a Luddite wearing fabric woven on a mechanized loom. In the year 2000, T.S. Stobart read something online while visiting a friend who owns a computer.

"It was Harold Pinter's obituary," Stobart said. "It was painful. It was also painful to learn Mr. Pinter had died."

Memorabilia from T.S. Stobart's playwright efforts were displayed in the shop.

All other efforts to bring T.S. Stobart into the 21st century had failed, and understandably so. It would be hypocritical for a man who made his living peddling books to pander to the technological enemies outside his door. And his disdain for that technology approaches the radicalism of the 19th-century Luddites.

"Some friends of mine brought a computer in here for me several months ago," he said. "I said, 'There are two things that can happen here: You can carry it out to your car, or I can bust it up with an axe.'"

The state's oldest book store

T.S. Stobart, a native of the Wheeling area, was an ex-hippie who owned and operated West Virginia's oldest bookstore. That was accidental. He wanted to be a playwright, and Tom headed to New York after a year of studies at Bethany College with great aspirations. And he returned to Wheeling to be "a big fish in a little pond."

Regular customers like Harold Gene Vitalie knew how to navigate the unique shelving practices of T.S. Stobart in his Paradox Bookstore.

His passion for theater came from being kissed by Katharine Hepburn at the age of 14. His fourth-grade teacher took him to the Big Apple to see Hepburn on stage, and afterwards Tom lined up for an opportunity to get a passing glance of the actress. Perhaps, in his wildest dreams, she would autograph the program.

His grandmother had knitted a monogrammed scarf for Hepburn and beautifully wrapped it. Tom said the actress snubbed the adults in the long line of admirers but was drawn to his feeble offer: "Present for Miss Hepburn,'" Tom said as the actress passed his way.

"She took my head in her hands, kissed my cheek, and said, 'Thank you, young man,'" Tom recalled. "I didn't wash my cheek for a month after Katharine Hepburn kissed it."

He credited influential teachers for his interest in literature. "I had great English teachers," he said. "I was very privileged."

Tom's search for books as a young man took him to the Veteran's Exchange on 11th Street in Wheeling. The shop's primary product line consisted of gifts made by World War II veterans, but it also had a selection of paperback books, 15 cents each or two for a quarter. Tom spent many enjoyable hours rummaging through the books and then consuming their contents.

Tom noted that the exchange rented the building from a Mr. Eddie Yee, who operated a Chinese Laundry in the same structure. Tom said Mr. Yee had a peculiar sign in his window for those who dropped off their laundry after hours: "When store closed, please throw up under transom."

While living in New York City, Tom supported himself working in a bookstore. When it became evident the Big Apple was not going to embrace and reward T.S. Stobart, Tom returned to Wheeling. Veteran's Exchange was one of his first stops, where Eddie Yee was liquidating his stock of books. In 1974 Tom and a partner, Carl Rauscher, bought the inventory of 500 books for $300 and went into business as The Ultimate Paradox.

He kept the bookstore on 11th Street for four years, but as the neighborhood declined, Tom went looking for a new home. He found it in the Centre Market District, where he rented a portion of a building owned by fish magnate Joe Coleman. And there he stayed, operating under as The Paradox Bookstore.

"There wasn't much reason for the 'Ultimate' and when we opened the store down here, we called it a 'Paradox,'" Tom said.

Rauscher left the partnership soon thereafter, but Tom stayed with the venture while continuing his playwriting and acting efforts.

"If I had to have a regular job, I can't imagine a better one than this," he told me. Still, he wished there were more traffic through doors, more sales, and more recognition of his talent as a playwright.

T.S. Stobart was a regional phenomenon whose works were produced by community theater groups in New York, Pittsburgh, the Akron/Canton, Ohio, area, as well as closer to his home at the Oglebay Institute and Towngate Theatre. The "StoFest" became an annual Wheeling festival of one-act plays named in honor of Tom, who wrote, directed, and acted in productions by the Independent Theatre Collective.

Inexplicably to Tom, his most popular play was "Ever After," which resonates with college theater groups and was produced off Broadway by the 29th Street Repertory Theater in New York.

"It seems to have a universal appeal," Tom said. "It's a sad, true story. When I first wrote it, I thought nobody would be interested in this because it's so specific about me and a lady, it would have no appeal."

The heartbreak of romantic love ran through Tom's plays like stains in in a coffee shop paperback. "You get involved with a lady, and your heart is going to be broken. I write sad love stories," Tom said.

He wrote a dozen or so of these full-length stories for the stage, plus numerous one-acts, but by 2010, Tom rarely wrote.

"I finally became discouraged," he said, chewing on an orange toothpick.

He was, likewise, discouraged with the state of the bookstore trade, hammered by recession and technology and the electronic generation's indifference to printed books, history, and culture. Tom told incredulous stories of cultural ignorance played out between these stacks, like the younger friend who had no idea who Johnny Carson was. Accordingly, the friend wondered if the iconic late-night television figure was some relative of Tom's because Carson's passing saddened him. In another case of generational and cultural history disconnect, Tom cringed when he was typing in the back room of his store and heard a teenage girl ask her father, "What's that guy doing?"

Certain adult customers tested his patience, as well. "People ask, 'Can you do any better?' Sure, I can do better. I can double the price and do a lot better for myself," he quipped.

Tom priced most of his used stock between $1 and $5. A large green bookcase with glass doors held the pricier books, like an autographed copy of Jim Comstock's *Best of Hillbilly* anthology. This bookcase was guarded by an attack chipmunk, which, according to Tom, was there to bite people who attempted to walk off with a valuable tome. The chipmunk was real enough, although it had been dead for more than three decades. Tom found it stapled to a piece of wood left on his porch and decided the rodent deserved a more honorable memorial.

If a shopper had a problem coming up with cash for one or two of the 25,000 books inside the store, there was a bargain section immediately outside the front door. A sign proclaimed "during business hours the books on the porch are 50 cents each or 5/$2. When the store is closed, please feel free to borrow them or keep them and pay me later. If you don't have the money to buy books and need or want to read, help yourself. Donations accepted. The Proprietor."

If, after all that, the prices were still beyond reach, there was a free book exchange rack that Tom maintained just outside Coleman's Fish Market,

T.S. Stobart pauses by the front window of his Centre Market District bookstore, March 22, 2010.

where patrons could drop off and pick up free books, magazines, and sound recordings.

Tom obtained some of his stock from estate and library sales, but most of it came through the door in the arms of sellers in need of a few bucks or shelf space.

"I'm in search of books all the time. I'm in desperate need of classic literature, science fiction," he told me. "Westerns sell very well, Americana and local and regional histories, also."

No condensed books, no textbooks, no dictionaries, and no encyclopedias, however.

"You can't even give away a set of encyclopedias. These days, you can just go online and get the information—that Wikipedia thing. You don't have to touch those nasty books anymore. You can access just as much material in books, it just takes you longer," he said. "I think computers are killing literacy, especially those damn text messages."

The stock in Tom's shop was as eclectic as its proprietor, ranging from sheet music and vinyl recordings to books about religion and a rack of classic Playboy magazines, always in sight of the proprietor's perch.

"The public and accident dictate what I carry," he said.

While books were arranged by subject matter, they were not alphabetized, which irritated many shoppers. "We love it when someone comes in from out of town and they ask if the books are in alphabetical order," said Harold Gene Vitalie, a retired high school history teacher who visited Paradox almost daily.

Harold shared Tom's disdain for technology and owned a huge collection of typewriters, but none he would share with Tom. He consumed three newspapers a day and countless books each year. "I stay away from computers; I don't know how to turn one on," he said.

Harold and Tom loved sharing stories about the customers and books who passed through this Paradox. A favorite tale is that of an oversized coffee table book of black-and-white erotic photographs of a French brothel and the dog that lived there.

"It was pretty classy, and I put $10 on it," Tom said.

The book languished on the shelf at that price, and Tom marked it down several times, until it hit $5, at which point, he decided to start reducing its price by a penny a day.

"Eventually, the entire front of the book was covered with price stickers," he said. "It finally got down to 36 cents and an old wino came in here, looked at it and said, 'This book is only 36 cents, I'll take it!' I'm closing up at the end of the day and propped up outside on porch is the book. He brought it back."

Tom finally sold it off his rack on the porch, presumably for 50 cents.

Tom could have realized a quicker sale and higher price if it were offered online. But such talk was heresy to Tom, who ignored other vendors' online sales to get a handle on the market and pricing. His method of determining a book's retail value was much more straightforward.

"I figure out what I got in it and go from there," he said.

Tom tried to compensate for declining sales by renting out rooms in his 11-room Victorian home and withdrawals from a rapidly declining inheritance from his father. Tom sensed that both his store and his health were in their twilights, with the prognosis measured in months, not years.

"I fear for the future a great deal," he said, then launched into one more bookstore tale.

"A playwright friend of mine was down on his luck and asked me if I'd be interested in buying a nice gray suit from him; he needed some money," Tom said. "He wanted $25 for it, and I said, 'I'll give you $25.' I wore it a couple of times, and then he had a preview of a play in Austin, Texas, and wanted to borrow it back. So, I let him use."

Tom had an opening in Pittsburgh and borrowed his suit back from his friend. Then his friend needed the suit when his daughter got married, and it once again exchanged hands. This lending went back and forth for a decade, until the friend died.

"His family called and asked me if I could be a pallbearer," Tom said. "I said no, and they wanted to know why. And I told them it was because he was wearing my suit. He was buried in that suit."

Playwright, poet, actor, and bookstore owner Tom Stobart died at the age of 66, August 4, 2020. He requested that his obituary specify his cause of death as alcoholism.

Tom's faithful customer from the day he opened the store, Harold Eugene Vitalie, died June 1, 2023.

A family friend, April Childers, assisted Tom with Paradox as his health failed. She brought it into the 21st century with a basic website and continues to engage in the business of selling used books at Centre Market District, 2228 Market Street, Wheeling.

The obelisk marking the grave of Dr. Simon Hullihen rises on the knoll of Mount Wood Cemetery in Wheeling. A grateful community raised the funds to purchase and erect the memorial to a beloved dentist and surgeon.

Chapter 12

Mount Wood Dentist

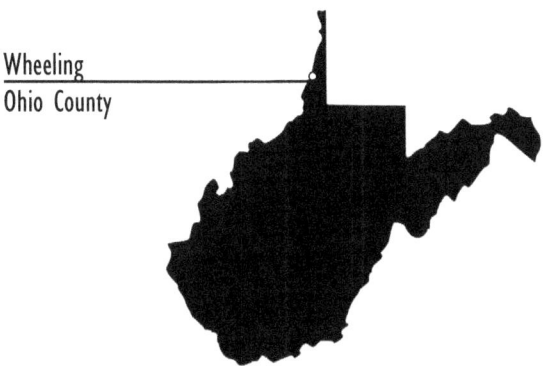

Wheeling
Ohio County

It is dusk and a dingy haze hangs over the Ohio River as the wide, brown serpent slithers into a den between distant mountains. I have a sweeping view of the legend and its urban child, Wheeling, from Section A of Mount Wood Cemetery. The spectacle and evening make me particularly grateful to still be on this side of the grass.

Adjacent to the Mount Wood Hebrew and Jewish Orthodox Cemetery, the rural cemetery is entrenched on Wheeling Hill, where Ebenezer Zane paused long enough to survey the landscape and declare that this place would become a land of promise. The valley, yes, but the hill was reserved for those whose promised land is just beyond the sunset.

Upon entering Mount Woods, I pass by a sign warning "Restricted Area Authorized Personnel Only." I assume, by virtue of being a mortal, I am authorized to enter, and I ascend the patched road of sorrow toward the summit, past crumbling, fractured headstones, the stumps of oak trees, and mausoleums inserted into the hillside.

Mount Wood is an example of what was a national movement in the mid-19th century, the rural cemetery. Replacing the crowded, urban-church

Mount Wood Cemetery overlooks the Ohio River at Wheeling.

graveyard, rural cemeteries featured carefully planned lots interacting with their settings' natural beauty. The rural cemetery thus became both a place to mourn and find comfort, to listen to both the sermons in stone and songbirds in the boughs.

"The flowers are beginning to bloom beautifully, and the shrubbery is showing forth its sweetest livery of green," stated a *Wheeling Intelligencer* article written in 1866. "In the evening, when the sun has gone down, and when the air is cool and pleasant, you can wander amid the tombs of Mt. Wood Cemetery and examine the monuments which mark the spot where different bodies are interred, or you can stand in the grounds and obtain a most excellent landscape view."

Little has changed in the ensuing 150 years, but Mount Wood has a tired and battered look this March evening. For all the planning and planting, everything feels crowded, stilted, and exhausted. Around the lower perimeter are the graves of the Jewish interments—the Finegolds, Katzes, Friedmans, Weissmans, and Malts. The concrete rectangles that mark their graves lean toward the distant serpent, as if pulled by the river's supreme authority over this land and all who would live and die upon it. Graves are

Perched on a steep hillside, Mount Wood Cemetery was a "rural cemetery" with carefully planned lots that interacted with the setting's natural beauty.

packed together so tightly one suspects the entire cemetery would slide into the river should just one corpse be raised at the final trump.

Above the Hebrews' graves rise the gaunt oaks, no doubt some of them among the 110 that were planted in 1933 in collaboration with Oglebay Park. It is unreasonable to expect even the mighty oak could withstand the buffeting winds, lightning, and erosion of this exposed face. The living deciduous cell, no matter how noble, cannot survive in a place where stone erodes and concrete gives way to the forces of gravity, ice, and time.

On the summit, however, the sense of security is stronger amid the towering obelisks, "white bronze" markers, marble stones, and mausoleums. The trees are more numerous here, so too the graves of the affluent, the famous, and celebrated Wheeling citizens of the 19th century.

The distinguished company in which I stand include Eliza Hughes, the first female doctor to practice medicine in the new state of West Virginia; Colonel Joseph Thoburn, a member of the First West Virginia Infantry and mortally wounded at the Battle of Kernstown; Noah Linsly, founder of Linsly Military Institute; Edward Norton, early city leader.

The most intriguing burial, by virtue of his epitaph, is the corpse of Dr. Simon Hullihen. Rare is the man who lives in such a way that the citizens of his city raise a marble obelisk to his memory and thereupon declare his death "a public calamity."

"Eminent as a Surgeon the wide fame of his bold original genius was everywhere blended with gratitude for his benefactions," states an inscription on one of the four base panels.

The stone, however, goes into no detail of what great deeds Hullihen (December 10, 1810-March 27, 1857) performed. The answer sleeps not in a grave on this knoll, but in the Wheeling Hall of Fame, where Hullihen's brief life is summarized as one of both "prejudice, scorn, and skepticism" and "bold, creative, inventive work and his tremendous contributions to mankind."

Dentistry in the era when Hullihen became a doctor was not considered a profession, and specialization was "tantamount to quackery." Yet, in Hullihen's time, he saw the Baltimore College of Dental Surgery open, and in 1843, he received an honorary doctor of dentistry degree from it.

His fame as an oral surgeon drew patients to Wheeling to seek his surgical intervention for defects of the mouth and head. He has been called the "Father of Oral Surgery," and rightly so. Hullihen performed more than 1,100 operations in an era when "neither anesthesia nor asepsis were in use." Patients with cleft palate, crossed eyes, and damaged lips and noses were given new leases on life through his pioneering surgical methods. Because he was developing the specialty as he went along, Hullihen invented many of his own instruments, and the designs of some remain in use today.

The growth of industry in the riverfront city brought with it many horrendous industrial accidents that required advanced medical care, but community leaders ignored Hullihen's demands for a hospital. It was only after combining forces with the Roman Catholic Bishop of the Wheeling Diocese that Hullihen was able to see the city's first hospital chartered in 1850. Worthy, then, is this man of his obelisk, the accolades, and a city's appreciation for his "tremendous contributions to mankind."

The haze becomes dusk, the veil falls upon the city and creates the illusion of down-river lights burning more brightly than before. My day of wandering has come to an end. The air at the lower elevation chills my skin and teeth as if death itself exhaled it.

My old tooth tingles in the chill. I must remember to call the dentist when I return home from wandering.

Bibliography

The stories in this work are based upon the author's interviews and interactions with the subjects, often over a period of several days or even years.

Background information for the stories was provided through *The West Virginia Encyclopedia,* edited by Ken Sullivan and produced by The West Virginia Humanities Council. It is available in both print (2006) and online at e-WV, https:www.wvencyclopedia.org.

Individuals interested in learning more about the encampment of soldiers at Dolly Sods, Seneca Rocks, and Blackwater will find documentary film *The Cliff-Scaling Soldiers of West Virginia"* by Robert C. Whetsell of interest. It includes an interview with Shirley Yokum and was released by the Augusta Heritage Center, Elkins, W.Va. Also visit the Seneca Project's website, https://thesenecaproject.org, and see the GOLDENSEAL articles by Robert C. Whetsell in the Fall, 2003 issue.

Index

Symbols

7th regiment of the West Virginia
  Volunteer Infantry 52
10th Mountain Division, U.S. Army 46

A

Akron, Ohio 55
Aleutian Islands 16
alluvial diamond 111, 115–117
Along the Way
  Chenoweth Covered Bridges 121–123
  Eye of Shepherdstown 31
  Filling Your Tank in Mabie 136–138
  Nelson Rocks via ferrata 72, 72–75
  Peter Shaver's Grave 108
Alpena 108
Annon, Clara Alice (Kirk) 78
Antietam, Battle of 30, 52

B

Baltimore College of Dental Surgery 156
Barbour County 91–95
Barrackville 84, 122-123
Barrackville Covered Bridge 122–123
Barron, Elizabeth 132

Battle of the Bulge 117
bears 66
Belgium
  Allied operations in 117–118
Bemis 102-107
Bemis Road 95
Bemis schoolhouse 97
Bethany College 145
Beverly 104, 121
Beverly-Fairmont Turnpike 122
Bikers for Christ 41
Bittenger, Donald 46
Blackwater Canyon 46
Bland, Byron 63
Bland, Erma (Harper) 63
Bland, Shirley. *See* Yokum, Shirley
Bland's Store 63
Bland, Stewart L. 63
bone cancer 133
Bonnell, Earl 102
B&O Railroad 122
Borrowed Time 135
  Hometown Boys 129
Bradt, Paul 45
Braxton County 40
brickyard labor 86
Brown, Dave 128
Buckland, Annie Grace (Jones) 111

Bull Run, Second Battle of 52
Burr arch bridge design 121–123
Butler Brothers 131

C

Calvin's Place 104–108
carbonated beverages 87
Carnation Milk Company 115
Carnegie, Dale 78
Carolina coal mine 85
Carson, Johnny 148
Cassity 129
cattle drives 52–53
cattle farming 51, 52
Cave, Gene 99, 102
Celtic harp 27
centenarians
   Shirley Yokum 62
   Silas Kirk 76-89
Centre Market District 147
Century Coal Company 94
Century No. 1 90–94
Century No. 2 90–94
Champe Rocks
   training ground 46
Chancellorsville 52
Charleston 106
Charlie the Miner 36, 37
Chenoweth, Eli 121
Chenoweth, Lemuel 121-123
Cherokee Sue 128
Chief Bald Eagle 48
Childers, April 151
Circleville High School 55
Civil War, American 30, 122, 155
   soldiers 52
Clark, Marvin 125, 135
Clarksburg 101
Cleveland Clinic 132–133, 135
Coal Country Miniature Golf Course 37
coal mining 40–41, 85
   closings 92–94
   deaths 94
   explosions 94
   scrap from 34, 36
   strip 93
coal-mining towns 90–94
Coalton 135
Coleman, Joe 147
Collette Gap 109
collie dog 53
Collins, Blanche 82
Columbia Gas 97
Company I 52
Connor, Carolyn 125
consecutive male births record 112
Consol No. 93 Jordan coal mines 85, 86
Constitution Avenue, D.C. 17
Cooper, Carly 67
covered bridges 121–123
Cross, Leon Dixon 139–141
Cross Roads Community Center 77
Cross, Tas 141
Cunningham Run 31, 34
Currence Brothers 129
Currence, Loren "Lodi" 129
currency, autographed tradition 105–107

D

Davis, Harold 41
Davis, Jim (Bryan Richard) 31–43
  broken back story 31–33
  childhood 40
  Christian faith 32, 41
  commissioned pieces 37
  metal sculptures 34–37
  music of 39–43
  origin of nickname 40
  strength examples 31–34
  weight lifting 40
  woodworking 37–39
Davis, Virginia Mae 35, 40–41, 43
Delauter, Amanda 91
dementia 88
Democrat 71, 83
Den Lin's Bar and Restaurant 91
dental instruments inventor 156
dental surgery 156
DeVry Institute 16
diet, high fat 89
Dolly Sods 13
  fires 57
Douglas, Jerry 131
Douglas John 131
dreams 79
Durbin and Greenbrier Valley Railroad 141

E

Eastern Panhandle 28
education in Appalachia 79
Elkins 97
Elmore, Chuck 128
Endless Horizons 75
Ever After play 147
Exxon 67

F

Fairmont 80, 82, 84, 128
family farms
  Davis 40
  Kirk 85
  Harper 66
  Yokum 52-53, 55
  Family Pride 131
Fansler, Homer Floyd 109
Farmington Mine explosion 40
farm labor 81
Fast, Betty Jean 78, 81, 86–87
Fast, Bonnie Louise 79, 81, 86-87, 89
Father of Oral Surgery 156
Faulkner, Charlotte Ann (Jones) 111, 116
Feather, Russell 118-119
Fike, Kathleen Ann (Kirk) 81, 86–87
Finch, Mary Margaret (Kirk) 78
First West Virginia Infantry 155
fishing 54
Flatwoods 40
flood, 1985 North Fork 61–62
footwear scarcity 80–81, 84
Ford dealership, Harper 69
Ford, Tom 53
Forquer, Mary Jane (Kirk) 81, 86–87
Fort Knox 128
Fort Knox Trio 128
Fulton, Robert 20

G

Galion, Ohio 113
game, wild 80
Gendarme 48, 49
General Electric 16
George, Harriet "Tippie" (Wiseman) 129, 135
German cemetery 17
German Street 29
Gettysburg, Battle of 52
Gilmore, Ellis 130
Gilmore, Margaret 130
Glady 95–107
Glady Creek 83
Glady Post Office 96–114
Glady Road 95
Good, Brooks 103
Grafton 127
Graham, "Little" John 128, 134
Grand Ole Opry 128
Grant County Ambulance 59
Grant Rehabilitation and Care Center 62
Great Depression
  bank failures 84
  poverty during 79–84, 103
Great Hall, O'Hurley's 21–23
  construction of 22–24
  policies of 25–27
Greenbrier Cooking School 57
Grover Jones Family Day 112, 115

H

Hall, John 75
Halloween 80
Hall, Virginia Mae. *See* Davis, Virginia Mae
Hammett, LaVonne 73
Hammett, Pierson 73
Hammett, Stu 73
Hammond Brickyard 86
Harley Davidson 41
harmonica 42
Harper, Ashley 67
Harper, Bardon "Buck" 66, 69
Harper, Cali 67
Harper, Carolyn 64, 66
Harper, Cole 67
Harper, D.C. 46
Harper, Harry 62
Harper, J.M. 64
Harper, Joe 63–71
Harper's Store 63–71
Harper, Stelman 62
Harrison Community Church 126, 131
Harrison County 31
Hebron Baptist Church 83
Heckel, Pee Wee 129
Hedrick, Frances 104
Hedrick, Susie 100
Henderson, Dr. Ed 119
Hepburn, Katharine 146
H & H Drug Store 84
Higgs, Veronica Fast 89
High Falls of Cheat 141
hiking trails 97
Himn, M.L. 65
historical marker 118
Hodginsville 128
hog pen 29

Holden, Dr. Roy 115
home remedies 64, 88
Hovatter, Margaret May 81, 86
Hubbard, Don 45
Huff, Tommy 137
Hullihen, Dr. Simon 152, 155-156
humor 40, 134, 141, 144–145, 150, 151
hunger 80
Hurley, Jay 14–27
  childhood 15–16
  merchandising philosophy 18
  metal working skills 18–20
  music 24-28
  travels 16-17
  woodworking skills 18
Hurley, Milburn Glenn "M.G." 15–17
Hussein, Dr. Mohammed A. 133, 135
Huttonsville 121
Huttonsville Presbyterian Church 121

I

Independent Theatre Collective 147
Indian ranger 109
infant deaths 78–79
IOOF. *See* Order of Odd Fellows

J

jam sessions
  O'Hurley's 25–28
Jones, Annie Grace 120
Jones, Buck 113
Jones, Dick 113
Jones family photo 112
Jones, Franklin D. "Sam" 113
Jones, Giles Monroe 113
Jones, Grover C. Sr. 111–115
Jones, Grover Jr. 113
Jones, John 113
Jones, Leslie "Arms" Howard 113
Jones, Paul 113, 118
Jones, Pete 113
Jones, William "Punch" Jr.
  diamond 111-120
  military service 117–118
  will 118
Jones, Robert 113, 117, 119–120
Jones, Robert (Sr.) 118
Jones, Rufus 113
Jones, Tom 113
Jones, Willard 113
Jones, Woodrow 113, 117–118, 120
J&S Grocery and Flea Market 91
Judy, Elizabeth (Yokum) 52
Judy Gap 45

K

Kentucky 128
Kentucky Jamboree 128
Kernstown, Battle of 155
Keys' Music 128
Kilarm coal mine 85
King Street 29
Kirk, Daniel Webster 78–79
Kirk, Darrell Willie 86
Kirk, George 88
Kirk, Howard Ezra 86
Kirk, John Mark 86–87
Kirk, Sandra (Orosz) 88
Kirk, Silas Hoover 77–90

L

Lambert, Wilmoth 101
lawn art 34–37
Levels Community 79
Lewisburg 119
Lilly, John 27
Lincoln Center 37
Lincoln Jamboree 128
Link, O. Winston 139
Linsly Military Institute 155
Linsly, Noah 155
loitering in post office 98–99
"Lonesome Fiddle Waltz" 125
Louis, Bonnie 81
Luddite 143

M

Mabie 125–138
Marbone Records 130
Marco, Jerry 135, 137
Marion County 80
Marshall College 67
Martin, Mary 128
Maryland 81
McDaniels, Dave 21
McMurran Hall 19
Meadowbrook Mall 125
Mechlenburg 17
Metal Lab 104
Mill Creek 128
Mollohan, Alan 106
Monongahela National Fores 45
Moorefield 52, 53
Moore, Sam 45

motorcycles 41
Mouse, Rebecca 52
Mouth of Seneca 52
multiple myeloma 132
music
    as family tradition 42-43, 103, 127-128

N

Nair, Roger 22
Nashville 132
Native Americans
    attacks on settlers 109–110
Nelson Rocks
    formation 73
    via ferrata 72–75
New River 120
New Tygart Flyer 139–141
New York World's Fair, 1940 112
Norfolk Southern 15
North American School of Travel 61
North Fork of the South Branch 45
    1985 flood 61–62
Norton, Edward 155
NROCKS 75

O

Oakland, Maryland 81
Oglebay Institute 147
Oglebay Park 155
Ohio 40, 55, 113
Ohio River 153
O'Hurley's General Store 13–27
O'Laughlin, Genevieve 21, 25
Old Jim 40

Order of Odd Fellows 29
Orosz, Bob 88
Osborne Brothers 129
Overstreet, Hazel 115

P

Packard Electric 130
Paradox Bookstore 142–151
Paradox, The Ultimate 147
Payne, Red 141
Payne, Shirley 139–141
Pendleton County 45-63
  cattle drives 52–53
Pendleton County Chamber of Commerce 62
Peora 41
pet cemetery 110
Petersburg 50, 53
Peterstown 111–120
Peterstown Cemetery 118
Philippi Covered Bridge 121–122
Philippi Races 122
Phillips, Boyd 129
Piedmont 67
Pinter, Harold 144
Pittsburgh, Pennsylvania
  mining companies 94
Potomac Highland Tourism Council 69
Potomac River 16, 20, 24, 51
  North Fork of South Branch 45, 51
poverty 77, 84
Princess Snowbird Legend 44-45
  Campground 44
Pryde, Jerry 137
public domain music 25

Punch Jones Diamond 111–120
  legal battle over 119
  sale of 119

Q

Quiet Dell 79–80, 85

R

Radford Arsenal 115
Radford College 114
Randolph County 95–107, 121
Randolph County Historical Society 109
rattlesnakes 46, 75
Rauscher, Carl 147
Red Sulfur Springs 113
Repair King 37
Republican 71, 83
Revolutionary War 109
Reynolds, Bertha (Kirk) 81, 88
Rhodes, Roy 101
Rich Creek 111, 116, 118
Rich Mountain 127
Rivesville 77, 89
Rizzetta, Sam 27
rock climbing 45–47
Roosevelt, Eleanor 119
Roosevelt, Franklin Delano 115
Rudy, John 86
Rudy, Mary 86
Rumsey, James 20
Rumsey steamboat 24
rural bar 104–108
rural cemetery movement 153–154

rural post office 95–107
rural stores 63-71, 95–107

S

Sadler Company 97
sawmills 97, 141
sawmill work 132
Scarbro, Missy Connor 125
School of Hard Knocks 128
scrap metal 34
Seneca Creek 45
Seneca Indian tribe 48, 54
Seneca Rocks
   deaths on 47–48
   legends 47
   military use of 47–48, 56–57
   walking path 47–49
Seneca rocks attraction
   tourism 69–78
   U.S. Government acquisition 51, 69
Seneca Rocks (formation) 45–48
   horse trails 51, 59
   pioneer climbers 45–46
Shaver, Francis 110
Shaver Mountain 110
Shaver, Paul 109
Shaver, Peter grave 108–110
Shaver, Sarah 109
Shavers Fork River 109
sheep farming 66
Shepherdstown 13–30
   eye of 29–30

market house 29
public library 30
welcome signs 20
Shepherdstown Women's Club 30
Shifflett, Calvin 95–107
Shifflett, Clarence 102
Shifflett, Dolores 131
Shifflett, Frances 100
Shifflett, Joseph 102
Shifflett, Maynard 102
Shifflett, Medford 102
Shifflett, Orville 102
Shifflett, Ronald 102
Shifflett, Rosa 102
Shifflett's Bar (Calvin's Place) 104-107
Shifflett's Glady Store 97–104
Shifflett, Titus 131
Shinnston 34, 37
Simmons, Lena (Wiseman) 138
Singing in the Hills 125–126
   origin 131–132
Sinks of Gandy 52
Sites, Anna (Harper) 63
Sites, Delzena "Della" 52, 63
Sites homestead 51
Sites, Jacob 51
Skidmore, Charlie 129
Smithsonian Institution 113, 117, 119
Snowbird (Princess) legend 44, 48–49
Sons of the Pioneers 128
Sotheby's Auction 119
Southern, Phil 37
Spaid, Clara Frances 81, 86–87
Spruce Knob-Seneca Rocks Rec. Area 45
steamboat 20
steampunk 143

Stobart, T.S. 142–151
  distain for technology 143
  playwright aspirations 145–147
StoFest 147
Strawder, Delbert 100
Swiger, Mollie A. (Kirk) 78

T

tepee 44, 60-61
Texas 117
Thatcher, Robert "Doc" 21
Thoburn, Col. Joseph 155
Thorn, Albert "Almost a Rose" 91
timber-frame 22
Tingler, Andrew 99
Town, Cheryl 129
Towngate Theatre 147
trains
  excursion 139-141
  logging 103
  mail delivery by 102
turnpikes, western Va. 121–123
Tuscarora sandstone formation 45, 73
Tyler 117

U

Underwood, Kimberly 129
unemployment 132
United Mine Workers of American
union hall 93
U.S. Bicentennial celebration 17
U.S. Department of the Interior 51

V

vandalism of graves 109
Vandgilder, Bessie 82
VanGilder, Everett 88
VanGilder, Marge 88
Veteran's Exchange 146, 147
via ferrata 73–75
Virginia Polytechnic Institute and State University 115
Vitalie, Harold Gene 144, 146, 150
Volga 93

W

Walnut Grove 86
Walter and Highland 84
Warner, Buck 69
Warren, Ohio 130
Washington 17
waterfall 85
Watson, Howard 130
Watson, June 130
Watson siblings 128
WBOY, Clarksburg television 129
WDNE, Elkins 128
weightlifting 40
Western Maryland 102, 139, 141
West Virginia Department of Arts 94
West Virginia Maneuver Area 46, 46–47
West Virginia Travelers 131
West Virginia Volunteer Infantry 52
Wheeling 142–151, 152-156
Wheeling Diocese 156
Wheeling Hall of Fame 156
Wheeling Hill 153

White Rock 48
Williams, Hallie 82
Williams, Hank 128
Willis Mountain Anticline 45
will protection 89
wintergreen berries 87
Winters, Pete 91
Wiseman, Ben 127
Wiseman, Benjamin 129
Wiseman, Birdie 127
Wiseman, Dorsey 124–138
    cancer battle 134–137
    childhood 127–128
    Christian ministry 135
    guitar acquisitions 128
    military service 129–130
    musical influences 127–128
    Nashville offer 132
    Ohio years 129–132
    radio & TV appearances 128
    spiritual leadings 132
Wiseman, Garrett 127
Wiseman, Harriet "Tippie" 129, 135
Wiseman, June 127
Wiseman, Lanora 127
Wiseman, Lena (Simmons) 127, 128
Wiseman, Mac 128
Wiseman, Margaret 127
Wiseman, Timothy 129
WMMN 128
Works Progress Administration 82–83, 114
World War II 56
W.Va. Route 28 73
W.Va. Route 33 45, 95
W.Va. Route 55 50, 53

Y

Yee, Eddie 147
Yokum, Adam 52
Yokum, Carl 44
    cattle farming 62
    genealogy of 52
Yokum, Carl & Shirley 44-62
    children 61
    romance 50–56
    wedding 55
    Vacationland development 44-62
Yokum, Esten 52
Yokum, Jack 61
Yokum, Patsy (White) 61
Yokum, Sam 61
Yokum, Sharon (Maluo) 61
Yokum, Shirley 44, 63–64
    awards 62
    entrepreneur 55–61
    genealogy of 52
Yokum's Store 58, 63–64
Yokum's Vacationland 43–61
    early cabins 54
    extent of 50–51
    restaurant 57
Yokum Tourist Home 56
Yokum, Virgil "Bub" 59

Z

Zane, Ebenezer 153
zip canopy tour 75

About the Author

Carl and back-roads traveling companion, Edison, who helped rescue him from the human pound.

Carl E. Feather is a seventh-generation Preston County resident; his fourth great-grandparents, Jacob and Mary Feather (Vätter), settled at Crab Orchard in 1803. The story of his German-Swiss Palatinate immigrant ancestors and their relationship to the Allegheny Mountains is told in *My Fathers' Land,* also by Carl. His book, *Mountain People in a Flat Land* (Ohio University Press), relates the story of migration from West Virginia to Ohio in the post-World War II years.

Carl is married to Ruth Evans Feather, a Certified Ophthalmic Technician originally from eastern Pennsylvania. Carl and Ruth have been Bruceton Mills, West Virginia, residents since 2020.

A retired journalist and professional photographer, Carl has freelanced for West Virginia's traditional life magazine, *GOLDENSEAL,* since the mid-1980s, and more than 100 of his stories have been published on its pages. He continues to write and shoot for the quarterly. His *Backroads* feature has been a staple of the magazine since 2004.

Wander More W.Va Back-Roads

If you enjoyed this book, please consider the other titles in this series, as well as *My Fathers' Land,* and Carl's books about another aspect of Appalachia—Ashtabula County, Ohio. All books in this series are available in high-quality editions from our online bookstore at books.by/feather-cottage-media.

To subscribe to GOLDENSEAL magazine, visit the West Virginia Department of Arts, Culture & History website: https://wvculture.org/discover/publications/goldenseal/.

Other books in this series:

Wandering Back-Roads West Virginia
Even More Wandering Back-Roads West Virginia
Still More Wandering Back-Roads West Virginia
Wandering Tucker County West Virginia (2025)
(all with Carl E. Feather)
Wandering Route 50 West Virginia (2026)

As an independent author and publisher, reviews are our lifeline to attracting new readers.

Please support our work by reviewing our books on amazon.com

order your books from our online bookstore:
books.by/feather-cottage-media

www.ingramcontent.com/pod-product-compliance
Lightning Source LLC
Chambersburg PA
CBHW070803100426
42742CB00012B/2238